INSIDE THE
SUGAR
INDUSTRY

by M. M. Eboch

Content Consultant

José Alvarez

Adjunct and Emeritus Professor
Everglades Research & Education Center
University of Florida

Essential Library

An Imprint of Abdo Publishing | abdopublishing.com

abdopublishing.com

Published by Abdo Publishing, a division of ABDO, PO Box 398166, Minneapolis, Minnesota 55439. Copyright © 2017 by Abdo Consulting Group, Inc. International copyrights reserved in all countries. No part of this book may be reproduced in any form without written permission from the publisher. Essential Library™ is a trademark and logo of Abdo Publishing.

Printed in the United States of America, North Mankato, Minnesota
102016
012017

Cover Photo: Prisma/SuperStock
Interior Photos: Shutterstock Images, 4, 21, 26, 30, 36–37, 54, 61, 68; David R. Frazier/Science Source, 6, 96–97; Hywit Dimyadi/Shutterstock Images, 10–11; Amihai Mazar/Hebrew University/Getty Images, 14; Science Source, 18; Red Line Editorial, 20, 52; Nathaniel Minor/Minnesota Public Radio/AP Images, 22; Nataliia Zhekova/Shutterstock Images, 25; Jeffrey Rasmussen/Shutterstock Images, 32; iStockphoto, 35; Buyenlarge/Getty Images, 42; Sam Owens/The Tampa Bay Times/AP Images, 45; Daniel Acker/Bloomberg/Getty Images, 48; Richard Drew/AP Images, 51; Suzanne Tucker/Shutterstock Images, 56; Science Picture Co/Science Source, 58; Southern Illinois University/Science Source, 64; Jorge Moro/Shutterstock Images, 66; Rodger Mallison/Fort Worth Star-Telegram/MCT/Getty Images, 71; Nury Hernandez/New York Post Archives/NYP Holdings, Inc./Getty Images, 75; Hulton Archive/Getty Images, 77; Chris Ratcliffe/Bloomberg/Getty Images, 78; Rob Griffith/AP Images, 82; John Epperson/Denver Post/AP Images, 84; Luis Alvarez/AP Images, 86; Universal Images Group/Getty Images, 89; Richard B. Levine/Newscom, 94

Editor: Arnold Ringstad
Series Designer: Craig Hinton

Publisher's Cataloging-in-Publication Data

Names: Eboch, M. M., author.
Title: Inside the sugar industry / by M. M. Eboch.
Description: Minneapolis, MN : Abdo Publishing, 2017. | Series: Big business |
    Includes bibliographical references and index.
Identifiers: LCCN 2016945206 | ISBN 9781680783742 (lib. bdg.) |
    ISBN 9781680797275 (ebook)
Subjects: LCSH: Sugarcane trade--Juvenile literature. | Sweetener
    industry--Juvenile literature. | Sugar products--Juvenile literature.
Classification: DDC 338.4--dc23
LC record available at http://lccn.loc.gov/2016945206

Contents

1 Fueled by Sugar 4

2 The Rise of Sugarcane 14

3 A New Source of Sweetness 26

4 The Science of Sweet 32

5 Selling Sugar 42

6 Sugar and Health 54

7 Facing Off against Other Sweeteners 66

8 A Sweet World 78

9 Healthy Land, Healthy People 86

Sugarcane Production 2014 96

Timeline 98

Essential Facts 100

Glossary 102

Additional Resources 104

Source Notes 106

Index 110

About the Author 112

1 | FUELED BY SUGAR

People often think of sugar as a quick source of energy in food. It is a commonly added ingredient to candy, sodas, and other snacks, making them taste sweeter. But in Brazil, sugar plays a more critical role. The nation produces fuel made from sugarcane by the billions of gallons. This fuel powers the majority of Brazil's cars. Along with domestic oil production, sugarcane has helped Brazil become energy independent.

In addition to energy independence, Brazil's sugar-powered fuel has another benefit. It is better for the environment. When the fuel is burned, it releases carbon dioxide and other exhaust gases just as gasoline does. The difference is that as the sugarcane grew, it steadily absorbed carbon dioxide from the air. The result is a carbon neutral fuel—unlike with fossil fuels, burning it did not lead to an overall increase in the carbon dioxide levels in the atmosphere. This has important implications for global climate change. More than a simple snack additive, sugar can have surprisingly wide-ranging effects.

Vast fields of sugarcane provide Brazil with enormous quantities of fuel.

Fuels blended with ethanol are widely available at gas stations.

ETHANOL

Ethanol is a fuel that can be produced from many plants, including sugarcane. To make ethanol, the plant material is grown and collected. Chemical processes turn it into ethanol, a clear, colorless liquid that can be used as a fuel. Ethanol contains less energy per gallon than gasoline does. However, when ethanol is mixed with regular gasoline, the ethanol helps the fuel burn evenly, which keeps the engine running smoothly. Unlike the gasoline that comes from fossil fuels, ethanol is renewable. The world will never run out of ethanol so long as people keep growing the plants used to make it.

In the United States, corn is the primary source of ethanol. In some other countries, such as Brazil, sugarcane is the primary source. Sugarcane is an ideal source of ethanol because it is so cheap and efficient to produce. When sugarcane is made into ethanol, the sugar is fermented. Extra water is removed and the material is purified. Sugar ferments easily so it can be turned into ethanol easily. In contrast, the starch in corn must be converted into a sugar before it can be fermented. This

Energy Booster

Sugar is a carbohydrate. Carbohydrates are the most important sources of energy for the body. However, sugar provides only a brief energy boost. Studies have shown that though eating sugar briefly increases energy, tiredness increases approximately an hour later. In contrast, walking rather than eating sugar created a longer period of energy afterward. A balance of proteins, fats, and more complex carbohydrates from whole grains may do more to maintain energy than sugar alone. Medical professionals also recommend small meals or snacks every few hours to maintain a steady energy supply.

Sugar to Ethanol

Plants make sugar through a process called photosynthesis. The plants take in carbon dioxide from the air, water from the soil, and sunlight. They create sugar and oxygen. This sugar can easily be turned into ethanol. However, using plant cellulose—the material in plant cell walls—is more complicated. The material must be treated to break down the plant cell walls into sugar. Then the solution can be fermented to ethanol. The extra step of breaking down the cellulose makes this type of ethanol more expensive than ethanol made directly from sugar.

extra step means it takes more energy to make corn ethanol than sugarcane ethanol. In addition, an acre of sugarcane produces approximately twice as much ethanol as an acre of corn produces.[1] However, sugarcane does not grow well in most of the United States, and the government's sugar policies make sugarcane ethanol unprofitable for growers. As a result, corn is a more popular source of US ethanol.

Most car fuel in the United States contains approximately 10 percent ethanol and 90 percent gasoline. This mixture is called E10. It helps reduce the use of gasoline. Most vehicles cannot use fuel with more than 27 percent ethanol.[2] However, some specially designed engines can use more. Flexible-fuel vehicles can operate on fuel blends with higher levels of ethanol, up to 100 percent in some cases.

Sugar could replace most gasoline in some parts of the world. In Brazil, this is already happening. Brazil is the largest producer of sugarcane ethanol in the world. Approximately half of the cars in Brazil are flexible-fuel vehicles that can use any mixture of gasoline and ethanol.

The remaining cars can use 18 to 25 percent ethanol.[3] Using flexible-fuel vehicles and sugarcane ethanol has reduced pollution in Brazil because ethanol is considered a cleaner fuel than 100 percent gasoline. This has been good for the environment while also reducing Brazil's dependence on oil imports. Abel Uchoa, a manager at a Brazil sugarcane company, says, "We see ethanol as the fuel of the future, whether it's in Brazil or in the world beyond."[4]

USING SUGAR WASTE

Sugarcane can provide a different type of energy as well. The sugarcane stalk has an inner pith that holds most of the sugar. The pith is surrounded by a tough outer rind. When sugarcane is processed, the stalk is crushed to release the sugar. The rind and the fibers from the center of the stalk become a waste product called bagasse. In the United States, sugar mills produce millions of tons of bagasse every year.

The sugar contains only approximately one-third of the plant's energy. The rest stays in the bagasse. In the past, bagasse was typically burned in the fields, causing pollution. Today bagasse is being used in new ways that reduce pollution.

Bagasse can be burned in a factory to produce steam, which can be used to generate power. Many sugar mills get their heat and electricity through this process. Some sugar and ethanol mills sell their excess electricity to the community. In 2012, Brazil got approximately 4.5 percent of its total domestic electricity from bagasse.[5]

Burning the bagasse releases some carbon dioxide. However, the amount is equal to the carbon dioxide that was absorbed by the plants as they grew. This makes using bagasse for energy carbon neutral. The process does not add additional greenhouse gases into the atmosphere the way burning coal or oil does.

MORE USES FOR BAGASSE

Bagasse can also be made into products such as plates and toilet paper. These products can replace items usually made from plastics or foams, such as Styrofoam. Bagasse products can be produced with less energy than these other materials require. They biodegrade in approximately 90 days, breaking down harmlessly.[6] Some studies have shown that using materials such as bagasse for paper products is better for the environment than

11

using wood pulp. Making bagasse products saves trees, water, landfill space, and electricity, while producing less air pollution.

In Brazil, several companies are using packaging that contains some bagasse. This packaging is made from approximately 30 percent sugarcane bagasse combined with recycled plastic.[7] Consumers can buy Coca-Cola and sunscreen in these environmentally friendly bottles. A few companies are also bringing this technology to the United States. In 2015, Coca-Cola announced a new "PlantBottle" to be made of 100 percent sugarcane plastic. The company says it plans to use PlantBottles for all its plastic bottles by 2020. Heinz ketchup bottles and plastic cups at SeaWorld are also using bagasse plastic.

Sugar in Brazil

Approximately 70,000 farmers produce sugarcane in Brazil. The sugarcane industry there is estimated to provide 1.34 million jobs. It contributes $50 billion to the economy each year and provides 16 percent of the country's energy supply.[8] Brazil produces more sugarcane than any other country, and the nation represents nearly 25 percent of world sugar production.[9]

Critics complain plastics made from plants are not as environmentally friendly as the companies might claim. Using anything a single time and then throwing it away is not ideal. Still, the companies maintain that these products will help protect the environment.

Sugar is often taken for granted. People stir it into coffee or tea to balance out bitterness. Cooks use sugar to make baked goods tasty. Ingredient labels show sugar in many other products, from breakfast cereal to yogurt. But sugar also shows up in some surprising places, from car fuel to dishes. Millions of tons of sugar are produced and consumed every year. It is a multibillion dollar industry for a product that affects nearly everyone's life, sometimes in unexpected ways.

Ethanol Ups and Downs

Ethanol has been used for more than a century. Brazil began testing ethanol in the early 1900s and required some ethanol in all gasoline after 1931. In the 1970s, Brazil attempted to reduce its dependence on imported oil. Ethanol from sugarcane was a major part of that plan. People used more ethanol when oil prices were high and sugar prices were low. When the reverse was true, Brazilian ethanol use fell. Starting in 2003, Brazilians could buy flexible-fuel cars. These vehicles can use different mixes of gasoline and ethanol. This helps protect consumers when the prices of gasoline and ethanol change. They can use either fuel, depending on what is cheaper.

2 | THE RISE OF SUGARCANE

Humans have long sought methods for sweetening foods and drinks. Ancient people in many cultures used honey. Beekeeping and honey production were common in ancient Egypt, Greece, and the Roman Empire. Boiled grape juice and dried fruit were also used to sweeten foods. The ancient Romans even used lead acetate, known as sugar of lead, to sweeten wine. Unfortunately, lead acetate is poisonous.

As much as people enjoy sweetness, sweet foods were not always a large part of the human diet. Honey and other sweeteners once were far more limited in supply than in today's world. Many people had to do without any added sweeteners. The discovery of sugar would change that.

Sugarcane seems to have first evolved in Southeast Asia. People may have cultivated sugarcane in Papua New Guinea as early as 8000 BCE. By 1500 BCE, sugarcane had begun spreading around the Indian Ocean and the eastern Pacific Ocean. However, the crop may have primarily been used as food for animals.

The remains of ancient beehives provide evidence for the historical use of honey as a sweetener in the Middle East.

In the 500s BCE, Indians learned how to refine sugar from sugarcane stalks. This made sugar better for human consumption. The technique spread east to China. In 510 BCE, the Persian emperor Darius invaded India. He learned about sugarcane, which he called "the reed that gives honey without bees."[1] The Persians kept the method of producing sugar from sugarcane a secret. When the Arabs invaded Persia in 642 CE, they uncovered the technique and spread it throughout their empire. Wealthy people enjoyed the new product, but the sugar industry involved brutal working conditions. Both the sugarcane stalk and the tools used to cut it were sharp and could cause injuries. In the Arab world, most field hands were prisoners of war.

Europe was largely unaware of sugar until the Crusades, a series of military campaigns carried out between the 1000s and the 1400s against Muslim forces in the Middle East. Sugar was first mentioned in England in 1199. Sugar does not grow well in Europe, because sugarcane needs mild temperatures. It had to be imported for European consumption. Demand was high, but supply was low, because much of the sugar spoiled during transportation. Sugar spread through Europe during the Middle Ages, but it was so rare and expensive that it was considered a spice rather than a basic ingredient. The price of sugar in London in 1319 was approximately equal to $50 per pound in 2016 US dollars.[2] In contrast, sugar can now be found in every grocery store for less than one dollar per pound. This inexpensiveness has arisen partially because governments in the United States and Europe heavily subsidize sugar.

A NEW ECONOMY

Sugar became more common after the 1400s. Christopher Columbus brought sugarcane to the Americas in 1493. The crop grew amazingly well on the islands of the Caribbean Sea due to the good soil, hot sunshine, and heavy rainfall. The Portuguese established sugar plantations in Brazil, where conditions were ideal for the crop. In the mid-1600s, Brazilian sugarcane was planted in the Caribbean. The sugar trade boomed. When the British conquered the West Indies, they took over sugarcane production there and also brought it to their colonies in North America. All these plantations needed many workers. Many of the indigenous workers quickly died from European diseases against which they had no immunity.

The need for workers, including those in the sugar industry, led to the establishment of the transatlantic slave trade. Slave traders bought slaves in Africa in exchange for goods such as rum, tobacco, cloth, copper, and brass. More than 12.5 million enslaved people were shipped from Africa

Sugar Heals Sickness?

When sugar spread to India, it was used as a medicine for ailments such as headaches and stomach flutters. In 1715, a doctor recommended a powdered mix of sugar, pearl, and gold blown into the eye as a cure for eye problems. A London physician's guide in 1769 included sugar as part of a cure for diarrhea. Sugar may have been seen as a medicine in part because it was so rare and therefore valuable.

The history of sugar production in the West became closely linked with the history of the slave trade.

to the Americas between 1501 and 1867, when the last known slave ship arrived in Cuba.[3] Millions died on the voyages. Millions more died in the fields or during failed escape attempts. Those who survived faced harsh conditions and generations of slavery. Meanwhile, sugar brought wealth to the plantation owners and traders. Sugar was called "white gold," because owning a sugar plantation was like owning a gold mine.[4]

The governments where plantations were located benefited from taxes on sugar. This gave them an incentive to support the sugar industry. Even after sugar production expanded, the sweetener was primarily used by the rich, because taxes kept sugar expensive. In the United Kingdom, the sugar tax was removed in 1874. Then the lower classes started eating more sugar as well. Average sugar consumption grew dramatically through the centuries. In 1700, the average English person ate 4 pounds (1.8 kg) of sugar per year. By 1800,

The Triangle Trade

The sugar industry became part of a trading system known as the triangle trade. Harvested sugar went from the Caribbean and the Americas to Europe. Finished goods from Europe went to the West Coast of Africa in trade for slaves. The slaves went to the New World, where half of them worked on sugar plantations. The three major trading centers—Europe, Africa, and the Americas—made up the points of the triangle. The triangle trade encouraged racism and enslavement for financial gain. The need for cheap labor led to powerful Europeans deciding Africans were inferior, to justify slavery. Eric Williams, a politician and historian from Trinidad, says, "Slavery was not born of racism; rather, racism was the consequence of slavery."[5]

the number had increased to 18 pounds (8.2 kg) per year, and by 1900, it was 100 pounds (45.4 kg) per year.[6] Sugar had become a standard part of the diet in many places around the world.

PRODUCING SUGAR

Sugar has come a long way since its early days as a rarity. As of 2014, sugarcane was the third most valuable crop in the world after cereal grains and rice. Sugarcane fields cover more than 10,000 square miles (25,900 sq km) of land around the world.[7] Approximately

How Much Sugar?

It is no surprise that some foods, such as soda and candy bars, are high in sugar. In other foods, the sugar content may not be as obvious. Breakfast cereals vary greatly in sugar content, from less than 1 teaspoon of sugar per 100 grams to more than 10 teaspoons. Here are some common foods with their typical sugar content.

Food	Sugar Content
Candy bar	6.75 teaspoons
Soda	8.25 teaspoons
Sweetened cereal	10.5 teaspoons
Unsweetened cereal	0.1 teaspoons
Banana	3 teaspoons (per 100 g)
Tomato	0.7 teaspoons (per 100 g)
Chocolate chip muffin	4.75 teaspoons[8]

Today's sugarcane harvesting is done with large, mechanized equipment.

190 million short tons (172 million metric tons) of sugar are produced worldwide each year.[9] Major producers include Brazil, India, Thailand, China, and the European Union. The United States grows 8.8 million short tons (8 million metric tons) annually and is typically the sixth-largest sugar producer in the world.[10] Approximately half of the US domestic production of sugar originates from sugarcane and the other half originates from sugar beets, the other main plant-based source of sugar. In general, sugarcane is grown in warm climates and sugar beets are grown in cooler climates. Thus, the main sugarcane producing US states are Florida and Louisiana, whereas the main sugar beet producing states are Minnesota, Idaho, North Dakota, and Michigan. Worldwide, approximately 80 percent of all sugar comes from sugarcane, with the remainder coming from sugar beets.[11] The main sugar beet producers are the European Union, the United States, Russia, Turkey, Ukraine, Iran, Japan, and China.

The production of sugarcane has advanced with new technology. The plant still grows best in tropical or subtropical climates with lots of sun and rain. Multiple crops are grown from a single planting. The first harvest is known as plant cane,

Types of Sugar

The most common table sugar is white sugar. It can come from either sugarcane or sugar beets. When sugar is refined, the plant juice is separated into sucrose crystals and molasses. At this stage, the minimally refined sugar crystals are brown sugar. They are further refined into white sugar. Molasses can also be added to white sugar to make it brown sugar. White sugar may be formed into different sized crystals. Granulated sugar is a common form for baking and adding to drinks. Very tiny, dustlike crystals are called icing sugar, powdered sugar, or confectioners' sugar.

and subsequent ones are called ratoon crops. In Florida, for instance, three to five ratoon crops are typically harvested. It takes between 6 and 24 months for the cane to reach maturity, depending on the location. The average time to maturity is 12 months. When mature, sugarcane is 20 feet (6 m) tall and looks similar to bamboo.[12] During harvest, the stems are cut but the roots are left behind so the plant will grow again. Sugarcane is usually harvested during the dry season, but in some places harvest can happen nearly year-round.

The harvested sugarcane is taken to a factory, where the cane juice is extracted. Often, large roller mills crush the cane, squeezing out the sweet juice. The cane fiber is removed and may be burned to provide the factory's energy. The juice then needs to be cleaned of dirt and plant particles. This might be done with slaked lime, a chalky product that can come from limestone. The lime causes the dirt and other impurities to settle. The cane juice is then boiled to thicken it into a syrup.

To form sugar crystals, the cane syrup is boiled again in large pans. The addition of some sugar dust, or very tiny sugar particles, will encourage new sugar crystals to grow. Finally, a centrifuge spins the mixture to separate the sugar crystals from the remaining liquid. The sugar crystals, which are sticky and brown, may be further refined before use. The residue of the sugar juice is molasses, a thick dark syrup. Molasses can be used in baking, made into alcohol, or fed to cattle.

At a refinery, raw sugar is transformed into other types of sugar, such as white or brown. This may involve washing and dissolving the sugar crystals, filtering the liquid, and then concentrating

Following processing, finished sugar is stored until it is shipped out to stores, food manufacturers, and other customers.

the syrup to form sugar crystals again. The sugar crystals are carefully dried to preserve them. Screens separate out various sizes of sugar crystals and they are packaged for different uses.

The final products may be sold directly to consumers for use in baking or other consumption. Other sugar is sold to food manufacturers. They may add sugar to products as varied as bread, soda, and condiments. Combined, these sources of sugar make up the sugar consumed each year as part of people's diet. The amount people consume varies greatly depending on the country. People in India consume little sugar, approximately 0.18 ounces (5 g) per day. In the United States, the average person eats more than 4.44 ounces (126 g) of sugar per day, or approximately half a cup.[13]

3 | A NEW SOURCE OF SWEETNESS

Sugarcane is not the only source of sugar. The beet has been used as a food for people and livestock for many centuries. The leafy greens, which are similar to spinach, have been eaten since ancient times. By the 1500s, people were also eating the root. They cultivated the plant until the root took on its most common appearance today, a bulbous shape that is usually a deep reddish purple. Two centuries later, the beet was a common food in parts of Europe. Today it is eaten raw, boiled, steamed, pickled, or made into dishes such as soup.

One particular variety of beet, called the sugar beet, produces approximately 20 percent of the world's sugar.[1] These beets grow in areas with cool climates that may not support sugarcane, such as Europe and the northern United States. In addition, turning beets into sugar does not use nearly as much water as the sugarcane process. This makes beet sugar production ideal for drier countries.

The method of extracting sugar from beets was discovered in 1747 in Berlin, located then in Prussia

The sugar beet joined sugarcane as one of the world's primary sources of sugar.

and now part of Germany. A chemist named Andreas Sigismund Marggraf uncovered the secret of turning beet sugar into a form that could be used in cooking. Franz Achard, his student, perfected the means of extracting sugar from beets. The king of Prussia paid to set up a sugar beet industry.

Still, cane sugar remained more popular, even in Europe. That changed during the Napoleonic Wars (1793–1815). The British Royal Navy blockaded French ports to stop imports. Farmers on mainland Europe quickly grew more sugar beets to replace the lost imported cane sugar. The popularity of beet sugar was also helped by the abolition of slavery in the West Indies during the 1800s. Using paid employees instead of slaves increased the cost of cane sugar. Beets became the primary source of sugar in Europe by 1880.

VEGETABLE TO SUGAR

Unlike sugarcane, sugar beets grow in seasons. Sugar beets are harvested in autumn or early winter and taken to the processing factory. Factories usually run for four to seven months as the beets are harvested. During this time, factories may operate 24 hours a day, seven days a week. The beets are washed of dirt and the leaves are removed. Then the beets are sliced into thin chips to increase the exposed surface area. The beet slices are soaked and agitated in hot water in a large tank. This process, which lasts approximately an hour, is called diffusion. Much of the sugar seeps out of the beets, turning the water into a sugary juice. The beet slices are pressed to squeeze out additional water. The remaining pulp goes to a drying plant where it is turned into pellets for animal feed.

The beet juice contains chemicals from the beet skins, and they must be removed. In this process, called carbonation, small clumps of chalk collect the unwanted material. The chalk is removed, leaving a watery sugar solution. The juice is evaporated to concentrate it. The resulting syrup is boiled in huge pans to evaporate the water and grow crystals. From this stage onward, making beet sugar is similar to making cane sugar. The sugar crystals are separated from the syrup, washed, dried, and separated by size. The final products of the sugarcane and beet processes look similar, though there are minor differences. Molasses from beets is not as high in quality as that from cane.

Loving Beets

Beets contain tryptophan and betaine, natural chemical compounds that help create a feeling of well-being. They also contain boron, a mineral sometimes used as a medicine. Among other qualities, boron builds muscles and increases the levels of testosterone, a hormone related to sexual development. This may explain some of the mythological associations of beets. The ancient Romans thought beets and beet juice caused feelings of attraction. Aphrodite, the Greek goddess of love, was said to eat beets to enhance her beauty.

Sugar beets are
collected and
processed seasonally.

Sugar from beets has some advantages. Most important, beets can grow in a larger range of climates than sugarcane. In addition, the sugar in sugar beets is more stable than that in sugarcane. Sugarcane must be processed near the fields, but beets can be transported longer distances for processing. Beets are typically also cheaper to produce and process than cane sugar.

A disadvantage of using beets for sugar is that beets do not produce bagasse. Without this waste product to burn, a beet sugar factory must use another source of energy. Typically the factories burn fossil fuels such as coal, oil, or gas. Although sugar beets only produce 20 percent of the world's sugar, they are an important supplement to the sugar market because they grow in more places.[3]

The Molasses Flood

On January 15, 1919, molasses turned deadly. A steel tank 50 feet (15 m) high and 90 feet (27 m) in diameter had not been properly built or tested. While holding 12,000 short tons (10,900 metric tons) of molasses, the tank fractured.[4] The resulting 15-foot-(4.6 m) high tidal wave of molasses swept through Boston, Massachusetts, at a speed of 35 miles per hour (56 kmh).[5] It crushed buildings and sheared off a column on an elevated railway. Rivets popped out of the tank and flew through the air like machine gun bullets. Twenty-one people died and more than 150 were injured in what became known as the Great Boston Molasses Flood.[6] The rescue efforts lasted for days. A local hospital and its staff became covered with molasses as they worked. The city smelled of molasses for months during the cleanup. Fire departments pumped gallons of molasses from cellars, and people used chisels to break up the gunk as it hardened. A three-year legal case found the company, United States Industrial Alcohol, responsible. Boston began requiring an engineer or architect to sign off on construction projects. That practice soon spread throughout the country, improving safety.

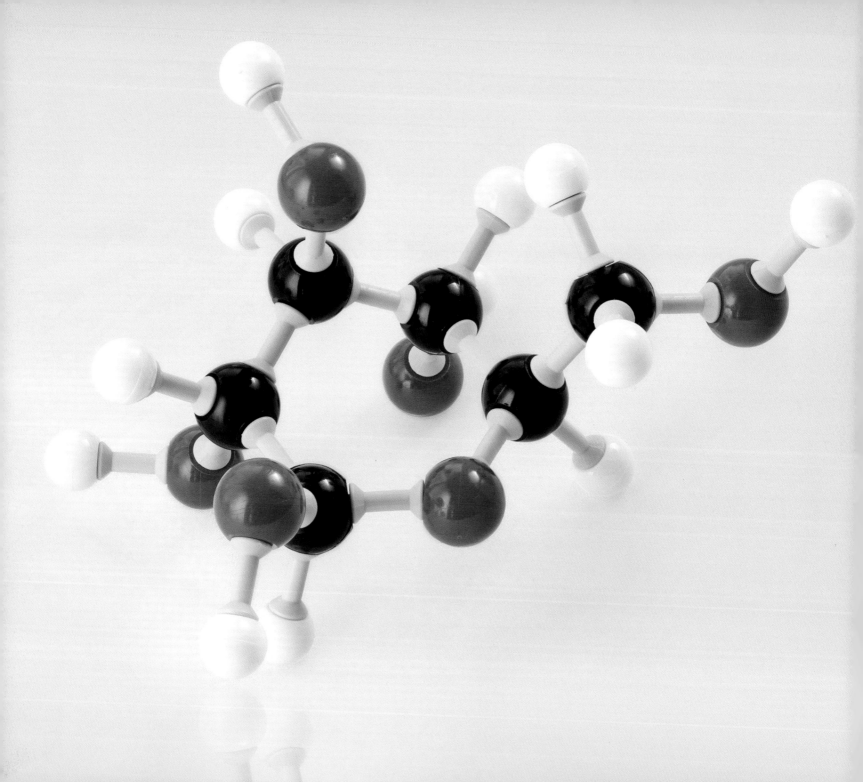

4 | THE SCIENCE OF SWEET

Sugar is a simple carbohydrate that is a source of calories and energy for the body. It comes in many forms, often with names that end in *ose*. Sucrose, glucose, lactose, and fructose are all natural forms of sugar. Sucrose contains a glucose molecule and a fructose molecule. It comes from sugarcane, sugar beets, and a few other plants. Glucose is found in many plant foods. Lactose is a sugar present in milk. Many types of fruit contain fructose. Fructose is also found in some vegetables, including onions, sweet potatoes, and parsnips. Food manufacturers often use fructose from fruit sugar in their products. It is a natural sweetener that is often less expensive than refined sugar. Smaller amounts of fructose give the same sweetness as larger amounts of sucrose.

Other natural sweeteners are honey and maple syrup. Bees produce honey from plant nectar. Maple syrup is formed when the sap of maple trees is boiled into a thick syrup. Honey and maple syrup contain both fructose and glucose.

Cornstarch can also be made into a sweetener. Products made from cornstarch include corn syrup, high fructose corn syrup (HFCS), crystalline fructose, dextrose, and maltodextrin.

Glucose, like all sugars, is composed of carbon atoms, black, hydrogen atoms, white, and oxygen atoms, red.

Dextrose is a type of glucose that can be produced from different forms of starch. Food labels may list it as cornstarch or corn sugar if it comes from corn. If the dextrose comes from wheat or rice, labels might list wheat sugar or rice sugar. Dextrose is found in many snack foods, desserts, and baking mixes.

Another category of sweetener is known as sugar alcohols. These come from plant products, with the carbohydrates altered through a chemical process. They may be found in foods with names such as sorbitol, mannitol, xylitol, isomalt, and hydrogenated starch hydrolysates. Some foods labeled "sugar free" or "no sugar added" contain sugar alcohols. Sugar alcohols may have fewer calories than regular sugar, but they still have similar effects on the body.

Finally, many artificial sweeteners have come onto the market in recent decades. These can be up to 1,200 times as sweet as natural sugar.[1] This means less of the sweetener is needed, reducing the number of calories in the food.

Healing Sugar

For thousands of years, healers have used dressings made of sugar or honey to heal wounds. The technique has gained followers in recent years, especially in Europe. Sugar may help heal wounds because it attracts water. As the sugar soaks up moisture, infectious bacteria are dehydrated. Drying out the wound may also help promote new tissue growth. While some doctors believe modern antibiotics are a better option, others claim sugar has worked on wounds that would not respond to anything else. Although sugar does seem to work, few studies have directly compared its effectiveness with more modern treatments. One study found honey more effective than sugar in healing wounds. More research might determine whether sugar deserves a place in medicine today.

Sugar's ability to dissolve in water makes beverages such as lemonade possible.

WHY WE WANT SWEET

Gums and mints often use sugar alcohols as sweeteners.

Most people find sweetness appealing. The apparent sweetness of a food depends on several factors beyond the amount of sugar. A food's temperature can affect how sweet it tastes. For instance, one study found that ice

A Revolutionary Food

Japanese scientists invented HFCS in the 1960s. Its use took off in the 1970s after further development. HFCS was seen as a revolutionary food innovation. It works especially well in packaged foods because it helps retain moisture, keeping cookies and other snacks soft. HFCS survives variations in storage temperature, which helps maintain the quality of soft drinks and condiments for long periods. HFCS can be found in many foods, including beverages, cereals, bakery products, processed foods, and some dairy products.

What Tastes Sweet?

Sugar may not be the only thing that contributes to sweetness. University of Florida taste scientists have been investigating the role of volatile compounds, chemicals that can easily become gases at room temperature, in fruit. These natural chemicals are found in very small amounts in the fruit. Strawberries are typically rated sweeter than blueberries. Blueberries actually have more sugar, but strawberries have many more volatiles. Researchers found that adding volatiles from strawberries to sugar water increased sweetness. They are not sure yet why this is happening. The volatiles may affect the part of the brain that perceives taste.

cream tastes sweeter when it is warm. Sugar can interact with other ingredients, heightening or muting other flavors. For example, sugar mutes acidity. Sugar is often added to tomato products such as spaghetti sauce because sugar reduces the acidity of the tomatoes. An individual's sensitivity to taste can also affect how that person perceives sweetness. Recent studies have found people have varying degrees of sensitivity to flavors. What tastes very sweet to one person may merely taste moderately sweet to another.

Sugar has several chemical properties that affect foods. It dissolves easily in water. This allows it to provide an even sweetness and texture to beverages. In addition, sugar lowers freezing points, the temperature at which a liquid turns solid as it is cooled. A lower freezing point helps prevent frozen desserts and freeze-dried foods from developing grainy crystals. For example, in ice cream, sugar helps keep the texture smooth. Sugar also raises the temperature at which a liquid boils. Candy making depends on controlling the crystallization of sugar. The results of this crystallization process change based on the boiling point. Soft products such as fudge require minimal crystallization. Hard candies result from extensive crystallization.

Sugar affects the texture of baked goods too. The yeast that causes bread to rise feeds on sugar for its growth. Baked goods also rise because of the presence of gluten, a mixture of proteins in cereal grains. Sugar helps control the development of gluten so the bread rises the correct amount and does not become tough. Sugar affects the color of baked goods as well. The sugar caramelizes, turning baked goods golden brown. Meanwhile, sugar binds with water, which helps keep baked goods from drying out. For these reasons, even baked goods that do not taste very sweet may contain sugar to improve texture and color.

Finally, sugar can act as a preservative, giving foods such as jams and jellies a long shelf life. Sugar absorbs water, which causes any microorganisms to become dehydrated. Thus, sugar inhibits the growth of microbes that could cause the product to spoil. Research has shown that sugar also seems to have antioxidant properties, which help maintain the texture and flavors of canned fruits and vegetables.

HOW MUCH IS TOO MUCH?

Sugar in the diet may come from natural sources, such as fruit or milk. It may also be added at the table or come from manufactured foods that have added sugars. *Added sugar* refers to sweeteners added to foods during processing, as opposed to sugar that naturally occurs in a food such as fruit. Added sugars come in many forms. Honey, molasses, malt syrup, corn syrup, and cane juice are

Humans versus Animals

All vertebrate animals have tongues with taste buds. However, different animals have different numbers of taste buds. Chickens typically have approximately 30, humans have approximately 10,000, cows have approximately 25,000, and catfish have more than 100,000.[3] Having many taste buds benefits animals that need to identify poisons. Cows eat a variety of plants. Some plants are poisonous, so cows need to be able to taste subtle differences. Animals also vary in how they respond to the basic tastes. Cats, dolphins, and sea lions cannot taste sweetness at all. Sweetness typically indicates the carbohydrates found in plants. Because carnivores rarely eat plants, they do not need that sensitivity. On the other hand, cats have a greater sensitivity to bitter flavors. This ability allows them to identify rancid meat.

examples. There is little or no nutritional difference between these sweeteners.

Candy, desserts, energy drinks, and sodas contain a lot of sugar. Sugar is also an ingredient in many foods that are not noticeably sweet. Because sugar is found in so many foods, most people underestimate how much sugar they consume.

Sources vary on how much sugar a person should consume. The 2015–2020 Dietary Guidelines for Americans, produced by the US government, recommend people consume no more than 10 percent of their daily calories from added sugars. That would be no more than 200 calories a day from sugar for someone eating a 2,000-calorie diet.[2]

The American Heart Association recommends even less sugar. It suggests most women consume no more than 100 calories per day from sugar, which would be approximately 6 teaspoons (30 mL). Most men are advised to get no more than 150 calories per day from sugar, or approximately 9 teaspoons (44 mL). A 12-ounce (355 mL) can of soda has approximately 10 teaspoons (49 mL) of sugar. By this standard, a single can of soda would provide more sugar than a person should consume in a day.[4]

5 | SELLING SUGAR

The US sugar industry went through ups and downs in the 1900s. During World War I (1914–1918), many European farms were destroyed and food production was down. The US government encouraged American farmers to increase crop production to make up for the shortages. Prices for those crops rose temporarily but fell again after the war. Then in 1929, a stock market crash triggered the Great Depression. Prices for most goods fell dramatically, and many farmers went bankrupt and lost their land. The government attempted to help farmers by creating a financial safety net. This happened in several ways for different farm products.

The Jones-Costigan Sugar Act, passed in 1934, was the first sugar act in the United States. The act named sugarcane and sugar beets basic commodities, which made them eligible for inclusion in the earlier Agricultural Adjustment Act of 1933, part of the Depression-era economic recovery plan known as the New Deal. As such, they were eligible for government programs. US sugar policy continued after the Depression ended. World War II (1939–1945) brought sugar rationing. Because sugar was scarce during the war, people were allowed to buy only limited amounts. A government brochure claimed people did not really need any sugar. Magazines

Many US women participated in sugar-saving efforts during World War I.

43

The Territory of Hawaii

In the early 1900s, Hawaii was a US territory. This meant Hawaiian sugar exported to the mainland United States was subject to import taxes. Hawaiian plantation owners suffered financially from the taxes, which convinced many of them to campaign for statehood. A government committee decided the territory was eligible for statehood. The people in Hawaii voted 2 to 1 in favor of becoming a state. Then World War II interrupted the process. After the war, attempts to achieve statehood resumed. However, due to many political delays, Hawaii did not become a state until 1959. That year Alaska and Hawaii became the forty-ninth and fiftieth states.

and newspapers suggested that sugar rationing was a good thing, saying it would improve health.

The sugar industry decided to challenge the growing public perception that sugar was unhealthy and unnecessary. In 1943, companies in the US sugar industry founded the Sugar Research Foundation, renamed the Sugar Association in 1947. Still active today, the association states as its mission "educating health professionals, media, government officials, and the public about sugar's goodness."[1] A spin-off, the World Sugar Research Organisation, supports scientific research of sugar's role in food.

In the early 1970s, the sugar industry sponsored weight-loss ads claiming sugar was a low-calorie way to satisfy the appetite. One ad from Sugar Information Inc. recommended eating an ice cream cone before lunch, claiming "Sugar can be the willpower you need to under eat."[2] No research had suggested that eating sugar before meals aided appetite control or weight loss. Another ad asked, "If sugar is so fattening, why are so many kids so thin?"[3] Meanwhile, youth obesity rates were rising. In 1972, the Federal Trade Commission

US Sugar grows
sugarcane on
large tracts of land
in Florida.

US SUGAR CORPORATION

Charles Stewart Mott, the founder of US Sugar, got his start in business in his family's bicycle tire company. When he became president of the company, he expanded the business. In 1931, during the Great Depression, Mott bought a failed sugarcane farming and processing company in Florida. He renamed it United States Sugar Corporation and became its chairman, investing millions of dollars of his own funds. He revived the company and brought in experts to help develop varieties of sugarcane more suitable for Florida. Through the years, the company continued to grow and expand, investing in modern research and technology. Today the company is primarily owned by its employees and two charitable foundations set up by Mott. The Mott Children's Health Center provides children's medicine services in Michigan. The C. S. Mott Foundation offers grants for a variety of projects around the world, including those involving education and the environment. The company employs 1,700 people.[4]

Super Sizing

Some trends suggest Americans are becoming more aware of advice to limit portion sizes. Whether they are cutting back on total sugar consumption is a different question. Coca-Cola reported in 2015 that sales were rising of smaller sizes of Coke. In 2012, Mars Inc. promised to stop selling its oversized candy bars. Instead it would limit candy servings to no more than 250 calories.[10] However, some packages still contained two servings, allowing the company to get around this restriction. The same year, Nestlé promised to reduce the amount of sugar in popular cereal brands, but only outside of North America.

warned the advertisers to stop these claims. That did not put a stop to the sugar industry's questionable advertising. In 1976, the Sugar Association won a public relations award for its ads promoting sugar for energy.

Meanwhile, corporations began to realize that adding sugar to their products could increase sales. In 1949, the food company Post introduced Sugar Crisp cereal to the market. Its success inspired the company to release other sugary breakfast cereals, including Sugar Smacks, Frosted Flakes, and Cocoa Puffs. The cereals were advertised to children with cartoon mascots.

Companies also increased portion sizes in the second half of the 1900s. McDonald's initially sold 7-ounce (207 mL) drinks in 1955.[5] For more than 50 years, Coca-Cola bottles were 6.5 ounces (192 mL).[6] In 1955, 10- and 12-ounce (296 mL and 355 mL) drinks were considered king size. A 26-ounce (769 mL) bottle was called family size.[7] Today, common single-serving sizes are 12-ounce (355 mL) cans and 20-ounce (591 mL) bottles.[8] Single-serving 32-ounce (946 mL) drinks are also available.[9]

CHALLENGING HEALTH CONCERNS

The sugar industry faced another challenge in the 1970s. Scientists began to explore the negative health effects of consuming sugar. Doctors were starting to believe high sugar consumption contributed to diabetes and heart disease. Dentists were especially critical of sugar's effect on teeth. All forms of sugar increase the risk of developing cavities. Sugars cause tooth decay because bacteria on the teeth feed on the sugar. The effect is especially high for people who spend a lot of time snacking on sugary foods or sipping sodas. Many experts believed people, especially children, would get fewer cavities if they ate less sugar. The media reported these stories. Many consumers came to believe that sugar should be restricted, especially for children. Sugar consumption declined, and the sugar industry decided to fight back.

The Sugar Association created an ad campaign designed to change the public perception of sugar. The Sugar Association recruited medical and nutritional professionals. It paid for scientific papers that would challenge the link between sugar and disease. It hoped this would discourage the government from taking any action to restrict sugar.

The campaign worked primarily by raising questions about sugar's healthfulness. Science was still uncovering exactly how sugar affected human health. The sugar industry used this uncertainty to convince people sugar might not be unhealthy after all. The Sugar Association claimed the scientific research "is inconclusive at best."[11] The International Sugar Research Foundation (ISRF) even hosted a conference on diabetes in March 1974. It invited only researchers who would challenge the connection between sugar and diabetes. A conference review claimed "a large

ASR produces
some of its Domino
Sugar products
at a refinery in
Baltimore, Maryland.

ASR GROUP

Several common brands of sugar found in grocery stores are part of ASR Group. ASR stands for American Sugar Refining. Its brands include Domino Sugar, C&H Sugar, and Florida Crystals, among others. ASR Group claims to be the world's largest refiner of cane sugar. The company sources sugar from more than 40 countries, with nine refineries in five countries producing more than 6 million short tons (5.4 million metric tons) of sugar annually.[12] Its sugar, syrups, and other sweeteners are sold throughout the world.

ASR Group began in 1998 with a partnership between two Florida sugar companies, Florida Crystals Corporation and Sugarcane Growers Cooperative of Florida. Florida Crystals was founded in 1960 by the Fanjul family, which had been in the sugar business since 1850. Florida Crystals planted the first organic sugarcane in 1995. The company operates the largest biomass power plant in North America, powering its sugar operations plus tens of thousands of homes.[13]

amount of research is still necessary before a firm conclusion can be arrived at."[14] A major diabetes journal published the conference review.

Some members of the ISRF thought the organization should do complete and honest research into the connection between sugar and disease. Their recommendations were ignored. Instead the group only supported research likely to promote sugar consumption. The research was part of a public relations plan to convince consumers sugar was safe. The Sugar Association also supported research into the idea that other elements of people's diets, such as fat or total calorie intake, were responsible for diabetes, rather than sugar.

SAFE?

The Sugar Association also established a Food & Nutrition Advisory Council staffed by doctors and dentists willing to support sugar. The council put together a long document that claimed to

Ignoring Dental Advice

The sugar industry fought to avoid government regulation based on sugar's relationship to cavities. In 1971, the US government started a program aiming to prevent tooth decay. Research clearly showed sugar consumption played a part in tooth decay. A task force committee was supposed to set research priorities. Of the eleven members on the subcommittee, eight were also part of the ISRF. The committee issued a report that included many recommendations from the ISRF. Research that might harm the sugar industry did not make it into the final proposal. Although it was known that sugar caused cavities, the committee did not recommend reducing sugar intake. It claimed this was impractical. The steps the group did recommend turned out to be ineffective. For example, attempts to create an additive that would cancel the effects of sugar on tooth decay were quickly abandoned.

summarize the science about sugar. It was sent to reporters along with a press release titled "Scientists Dispel Sugar Fears."[15] The report was not labeled as coming from the sugar industry.

Meanwhile, the US Food and Drug Administration (FDA) was conducting reviews of food additives to determine whether they were "generally recognized as safe" (GRAS). Sugar was one substance under consideration. The committee contained two members who had received funding from the sugar industry. It also used the Food & Nutrition Advisory Council as a major source. In 1976, the committee declared sugar not a hazard to the public. The Sugar Association released an ad claiming "Sugar is Safe!" It declared, "The next time you hear a promoter attacking sugar, beware the ripoff. . . . Ask yourself what he's promoting or what he is seeking to cover up."[16]

NO LIMITS

Sugar's inclusion on the list of GRAS foods is significant. It means food manufacturers are allowed to add any amount to any food. However, the debate continued as to whether sugar really is safe, especially at high amounts. A government Select Committee on Nutrition

GRAS Status

According to the FDA, any substance intentionally added to food is a food additive. Food additives are subject to review by the FDA before the additive can be released on the market. If they are approved, they receive the GRAS label. However, substances that are already GRAS by qualified experts do not receive FDA review. In some cases, the FDA has accepted a manufacturer's declaration that their product meets the GRAS standards. The manufacturer provides evidence to back its claims. However, not every GRAS additive has been carefully studied by the FDA.

Soft drinks cups stand alongside their equivalent sugar content in sugar cubes at a 2012 news conference in support of healthier drink choices.

and Human Needs investigated the link between sugar, diabetes, and heart disease. The committee included a panel of experts from around the world. They claimed that differences in sugar consumption explained different diabetes rates. In 1977, the committee released a report recommending Americans lower their sugar intake by 40 percent.[17] The Sugar Association attacked the report. Eventually, government guidelines merely suggested people should avoid too much sugar, without clarifying how much was too much.

Calories from Sugar[18]

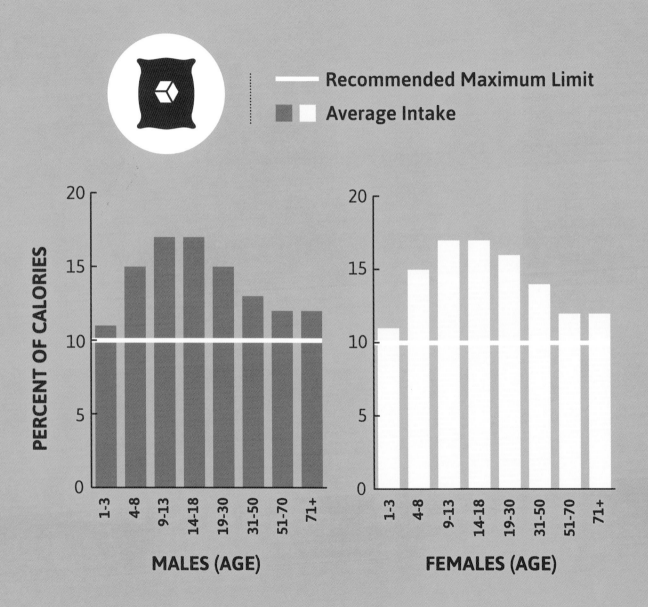

Recommended Maximum Limit

Average Intake

PERCENT OF CALORIES

MALES (AGE)

1-3 4-8 9-13 14-18 19-30 31-50 51-70 71+

FEMALES (AGE)

1-3 4-8 9-13 14-18 19-30 31-50 51-70 71+

Some research is again considering the health effects of sugar. Meanwhile, the sugar industry has continued to lobby against any recommendations to limit sugar intake. In 2003, the World Health Organization (WHO) recommended people should get no more than 10 percent of their calories from added sugars.[19] The Sugar Association president and two US senators supported by the sugar industry complained. They threatened to cut off funding to the WHO, and the recommendation was dropped from the official report.

Yet research continued, with more evidence pIling up against sugar. Many doctors and researchers continue to be convinced sugar causes chronic diseases that lead to death. Some researchers estimate hundreds of thousands of lives could be saved every year if people ate less sugar. Scientists and health-care professionals cannot agree on how much sugar can be consumed as part of a healthy diet. The sugar industry and food manufacturers take advantage of this ambiguity. They claim sugar has been declared healthy. In reality, the FDA and other organizations said something much different. They did not disagree with criticisms of sugar, but they could not say exactly how much sugar was acceptable.

6 | SUGAR AND HEALTH

Several medical associations consider the consumption of sugar a major health problem. For example, the American Heart Foundation claims added sugars "contribute zero nutrients, but many added calories that can lead to extra pounds, or even obesity, thereby reducing heart health."[1]

The relationship between sugar and health problems is not completely understood. However, sugar is thought to contribute to poor health in several ways. Sugar has calories but little other nutritional value. People who eat a lot of sugar may not consume enough healthful food. This can lead to poor nutrition.

In addition, eating high-calorie, sweetened foods can contribute to weight gain. In the early 1960s, obesity affected 13 percent of Americans.[2] In 2016, a study by the Centers for Disease Control and Prevention (CDC) put the obesity rate for US adults at 34.9 percent. The rate among children ages 2 to 19 was 17 percent.[3] Obesity-related diseases are the second-leading cause of preventable death in the United States, after tobacco use. Obesity can contribute to type 2 diabetes, heart disease, and cancer. It increases the risk of asthma, arthritis,

Sugar can cause health issues when consumed in excess. The question of exactly how much is excessive is controversial.

and depression. Obesity and the diseases it causes also affect individuals and the country financially. Every year, Americans spend billions on medical costs and lose many hours of work time due to the effects of obesity.

Many factors contribute to obesity, including diet and a lack of physical activity. Because these factors interact in complex ways, it is difficult to say exactly how each factor contributes. Still, many experts believe a large part of the blame belongs to sugary drinks and food. This is partly because people simply eat too much of them. These snack items are heavily advertised and are often served in large portion sizes. The average calorie intake among Americans increased by 200 to 300 calories per day between 1971 and 2001.[4] A report in the *American Journal of Preventive Medicine* claimed sugary drinks, including those using sugar and those using HFCS, were the largest single contributor to this calorie increase.

HEART HEALTH

A high-sugar diet can also increase triglyceride levels. Triglycerides are a type of fat that is found in the blood. High triglyceride levels increase the risk of coronary artery disease. This condition damages the blood vessels and can lead to heart failure.

Determining a single cause for a disease is often difficult, if not impossible. Throughout the 1900s, many health experts believed a high-fat diet was to blame for heart disease. Some other researchers claimed sugar was to blame. Most people thought the answer had to be one or the other, fat or sugar. In fact, both may play a part. Many health-care professionals recommend a

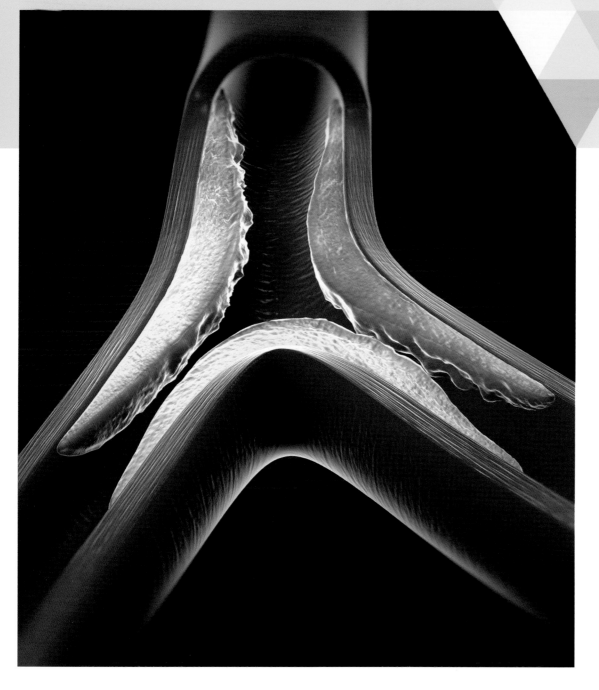

Scientists have
linked triglycerides
to atherosclerosis,
the buildup of
blood-blocking plaque in
the blood vessels.

low-fat diet, but the evidence is piling up that sugar also plays a role in heart disease and other medical conditions.

Today metabolic syndrome and insulin resistance are seen as major contributors to heart disease. Metabolic syndrome describes a group of risk factors that raise a person's risk for heart disease, stroke, and diabetes. These risk factors are a large waistline, high blood pressure, high blood sugar levels after fasting, a low level of high-density lipoprotein (HDL) cholesterol, and a high level of triglycerides. In the United States, 75 percent of the money spent on health care goes to treating metabolic problems and their resulting diseases.[5] Insulin resistance is a condition in which the body does not effectively use insulin, a hormone that helps the body absorb glucose for energy. Glucose builds up in the blood instead of being absorbed by the cells. Insulin resistance

Metabolism

Food consists of carbohydrates, proteins, and fats. The body uses the process of metabolism to get energy from food. The digestive system contains chemicals that break the food into sugars and acids. The body may immediately use these as fuel. It can also store the energy in body fat, muscles, or the liver for later use. People develop metabolic disorders if their body does not properly process nutrients. The effects of metabolic disorders may be mild, serious, or even life-threatening. Some metabolic disorders are genetic, passed down through families. For example, some babies are born without enough of the enzyme that breaks down the sugar in milk. These conditions are usually identified through early testing. People with such conditions may have to follow special diets or take medications throughout life. Other metabolic disorders can be developed over time through unhealthy habits, such as a poor diet and lack of exercise. Type 2 diabetes is an example of one of these.

is thought to contribute to obesity, heart disease, and type 2 diabetes. Insulin resistance may also contribute to many cancers.

Diabetes is a disease in which blood sugar levels are consistently too high. Diabetes can lead to heart disease and stroke. It can also damage the eyes, kidneys, and nerves, and lead to the need to amputate a limb. Many studies suggest consuming too much sugar can increase the risk of type 2 diabetes.

SUGAR IN THE BLOOD AND LIVER

The body uses carbohydrates, including sugar, for energy. Blood sugar is the type of sugar that circulates in human blood. It is in the form of glucose and is an important source of energy for cells. However, in time, excessively high levels of blood sugar can cause serious health problems. Blood sugar rises when someone eats too much food, especially food high in carbohydrates. Inactivity, some medications, stress, dehydration, and illness can also increase blood sugar levels.

The type of sugar consumed also affects the body. Glucose and fructose are both sugars, but the body processes them differently. Glucose is metabolized by every cell in the body. Fructose is primarily metabolized by the liver. Consuming 100 calories of table sugar will affect the body differently than consuming 100 calories of rice or potatoes. The table sugar is made up of equal amounts of glucose and fructose. The rice and potatoes are primarily glucose. The liver must work harder to metabolize fructose. The liver must also work harder when someone consumes sugar in liquid form, such HFCS in soda or juice. HFCS contains a higher percentage of fructose than

Most soft drinks sold today use HFCS as a sweetener.

How the Tongue Tastes

Taste buds on the tongue contain clusters of taste receptor cells. A network of sensory nerve fiber endings is woven among the taste receptor cells. The taste receptor cells stimulate the nerve fiber endings through the release of chemicals. This stimulation travels through the nerves to the brain. The brain responds by identifying five primary flavors. These are sweet, salty, sour, bitter, and umami, a savory taste found in meats, cheese, and many other products. Smell plays a larger role in determining subtleties of taste. Appearance also affects the way food tastes. Studies have shown people have a harder time identifying flavors if they cannot see and identify the food.

table sugar contains. For this reason, many people consider it less healthful.

Studies of lab rats and mice show their livers convert high levels of fructose to fat. Excess fat in the liver is associated with insulin resistance and metabolic syndrome. When lab animals were fed sugar at levels similar to what Americans consume, insulin resistance and metabolic syndrome developed in a matter of months. The fatty liver and insulin resistance went away after the lab animals stopped consuming sugar.

It is difficult to say for certain whether humans are affected the same way as lab animals. To obtain accurate results, dietary studies should last for months or years. Participants must carefully follow the diet and accurately report what they consume. Conducting studies in this way is difficult. Scientists cannot keep people in a controlled setting for months or years. Meanwhile, most people are not willing or able to precisely track the exact amount of everything they eat and drink.

SUGAR ADDICTION

Scientists from the University of California, San Francisco (UCSF) released an article in 2012 titled "The Toxic Truth about Sugar." They suggested sugar should be regulated in the way alcohol and tobacco are. These scientists cited studies suggesting sugar is addictive. With an addiction, a person does not have control over what he or she is eating, using, or taking. The UCSF scientists believe eating sugar can cause that lack of control.

When sugar touches the tongue, the taste buds send a pleasure signal to the brain. Sugar stimulates the pleasure centers of the brain to a much stronger degree than other tasty foods. This pleasure response encourages people to eat more sugar. In prehistoric times, people likely

What Is Addiction?

The term *addiction* was once used only in reference to substances that alter the chemical balance of the brain. By this definition, alcohol, tobacco, illegal drugs, and some prescription drugs can cause addiction. Today most health-care professionals believe in a broader definition of addiction. They note psychological dependency may also be an addiction. If a person has trouble controlling how much they do something and becomes dependent on that thing, they may have an addiction. People can be addicted to many things, including gambling, sex, the Internet, and work. Even a good habit, such as exercise, may become an addiction. A habit is done by choice; a person with an addiction is not able to control his or her behavior without help. He or she may need the substance or activity more often, in larger doses, to receive the same pleasures. The person suffers if the substance or activity is withdrawn. Addictive behavior can cause feelings of shame, guilt, hopelessness, or anxiety. It may lead to problems socially or at school, home, or work. Treatments for addiction include counseling and medication.

Taste buds and the signals they send to the brain have a significant impact on human eating patterns.

needed all the sugar they could find. Naturally sweet foods such as fruit were healthy, and people who spent their days hunting or gathering needed the calories. The brain's pleasure signals were a reward for consuming beneficial food. Today the brain reacts in the same way, even though sweet foods are much easier to find. Sugar affects the hormones that tell the brain whether it is hungry or satisfied. With sugar, the more people eat, the less likely they are to realize they have had enough. Instead, consuming sugar creates a desire for even more sugar.

Science does not yet understand exactly how sugar affects all parts of the body. Still, many studies suggest sugar can be dangerous to health, and many health experts recommend people eat less of it. If the public begins following these recommendations, the sugar industry may see a slump in sales.

7 | FACING OFF AGAINST OTHER SWEETENERS

When sugar faced criticism for its health effects in the 1970s, many food manufacturers did not want the word *sugar* at the top of ingredient lists. Fructose had the appearance of being more natural because it is the main sugar in fruit. Many people associate things seen as natural with health. Even though sugar also comes from plants, people could be convinced fructose was healthier.

One source of fructose is HFCS, a liquid sweetener made from corn. In reality, sugar and HFCS are very similar. Chemically speaking, HFCS is almost the same as sugar, and there are no major nutritional differences between them. In fact, HFCS was created to be indistinguishable from refined sugar when used in soft drinks. Still, the food industry promoted HFCS as a healthy alternative to sugar. In the 1980s, many food and beverage companies switched to HFCS as their sweetener. As a bonus to food manufacturers, HFCS is typically cheaper than sugar. In some years, US sugar policy causes the price of sugar to be higher than the world price of sugar. Meanwhile, US corn prices are subsidized by the

One of today's most popular sweeteners, HFCS, is produced from corn.

Many kinds of fruit are high in fructose, but they also contain other important nutrients.

government, keeping them very low. HFCS prices have remained lower than sugar prices, which encourages companies to use HFCS.

Then scientists began to realize fructose might be less healthy than glucose. Whereas glucose stimulates the body to release chemicals that regulate food intake, fructose does not. Fructose also seems to encourage the formation of more new fat cells. Although HFCS has only slightly more fructose than sugar, *high-fructose corn syrup* sounds worse because of the word *fructose* in the name.

Through the years, the sugar industry and the corn industry fought to control public perception over which was healthier. Overall, consumption of both increased greatly. The amount of HFCS consumed by the average American went from 0.5 pounds (0.2 kg) per year in 1970 to 43.5 pounds (19.7 kg) per year in 2010.[1] Much of this consumption comes from packaged foods sweetened with HFCS. Because both sugar and HFCS consumption rose greatly in recent decades, both of them have been blamed for the rising obesity rates. Because they are so similar, it likely makes no difference which is consumed.

DISPUTING DIFFERENCES

The fight continues, and words such as *natural* are often tossed around. In reality, both sugar and HFCS come from natural products. Some people have accused HFCS of being unnatural because of the chemicals used to convert cornstarch into fructose and glucose. In 2008, the Sugar Association petitioned the FDA to prohibit food manufacturers from using the word *natural* on foods that contained HFCS. The FDA agreed but then reversed its decision after the makers of HFCS protested.

In any case, whether something is natural has little to do with its healthfulness. In fact, many natural sweeteners have high levels of fructose. Concentrated apple or pear juices are almost two-thirds fructose. Raw agave nectar contains 90 percent fructose.[2] If fructose is worse for people than glucose is, switching from sugar or HFCS to these natural sweeteners will not improve health.

To complicate matters, there is no legal definition of natural. The FDA policy is that a food cannot be labeled natural if it contains anything artificial or synthetic that people would not normally expect to find in that food. For example, no color additives are allowed. However, the FDA does not consider production or processing methods. A crop could have been grown with pesticides and processed with chemicals and still be considered natural. By the FDA guidelines, both sugar and HFCS are natural. In 2016, the FDA asked for public comment on whether the term *natural* should be more clearly defined and, if so, how. In the future, rules for using the terminology may change.

BACK TO SUGAR

Backlash against HFCS has led to the increased popularity of sugar. In 2009, PepsiCo introduced a "Throwback" line of sodas sweetened by sugar rather than HFCS. Other companies also switched from HFCS to sugar, including Starbucks and Snapple. Many brands advertised "No High-Fructose Corn Syrup."[3] The status of sugar seemed to be on the rise again.

The Corn Refiners Association fought back with ads claiming HFCS is not any less healthy than sugar. When that failed to convince consumers, the industry group asked the FDA to allow it to rebrand its product as corn sugar. The FDA refused in 2012, on the basis that sugar is a solid and syrup is a liquid. Thus HFCS could not be sugar. The FDA response also noted that "corn sugar" had been used to describe dextrose for more than 30 years.[4] Dextrose is a form of glucose derived from corn. Changing the names would result in confusion and potential harm, according to the FDA.

A shift back to sodas with sugar proved successful, and in 2011 PepsiCo made them a permanent part of its product line.

The debates continue. In 2015, a scientific advisory committee recommended that the 2015–2020 Dietary Guidelines for Americans suggest people keep added sugars to no more than 10 percent of their diets.[5] The head of the Sugar Association, Andy Briscoe, waged a campaign claiming sugar is not a health risk. He suggested HFCS is worse. The Dietary Guidelines were released with the 10 percent maximum recommendation.[6] Now that sugar is being criticized again, some manufacturers label it as "evaporated cane juice" on food labels.[7] Regardless of the name, there is little health difference between sugar and HFCS.

....

What's in a Name?

Changing the names of common foods can be more than confusing; it can be dangerous. Some people are not able to tolerate certain ingredients, such as fructose. They need to understand food labels to make sure they avoid the substance. People who cannot tolerate fructose can still eat dextrose, sometimes called corn sugar, because it is glucose. The corn industry wanted to start using the term *corn sugar* for HFCS. Had they been allowed to do so, people who could not tolerate the fructose in HFCS might not have known what they were eating.

Sugar also faced a new challenge in the form of artificial sweeteners. Artificial sweeteners add sweetness without calories. They may also be called noncaloric sweeteners, sugar substitutes, or nonnutritive sweeteners. Products that use sugar substitutes may be labeled "diet" or "sugar-free."

Sugar substitutes are usually much sweeter than table sugar. For example, aspartame (sold as Equal and NutraSweet) is 220 times sweeter than sucrose. Sucralose (sold under the brand name Splenda) is 600 times sweeter than sucrose. Saccharin (sold as Sweet 'N Low, Sweet Twin, and NectaSweet) is 200 to 700 times sweeter than sucrose.[8]

All of these sugar substitutes are approved by the FDA as safe for people in limited quantities. Artificial sweeteners do not cause cavities. They usually do not raise blood sugar, so they are often recommended for diabetics. Less is known about the other health effects of sugar substitutes. The National Library of Medicine, a resource from the National Institutes of Health, suggests more research is needed. It notes that no clear evidence links the artificial sweeteners available in the

United States to diseases. However, there is also not enough evidence to know whether their use leads to weight loss.

Some sugar substitutes do have calories and may affect blood sugar. Sugar alcohols are carbohydrates that can occur naturally in some fruits and vegetables but can also be manufactured. They contain calories, but much fewer of them than regular sugar. Some sugar alcohols are less sweet than sugar, but they may be combined with artificial sweeteners to enhance sweetness. Food labels may simply list the term *sugar alcohol*, or they may name a specific type, such as xylitol. Sugar alcohols can be found in processed foods and other products, including toothpaste, mouthwash, and chewing gum.

Inventing New Sweeteners

Sugar substitutes are not new. The Japanese invented a syrup derived from starches in the 800s CE. A German chemist discovered how to make a glucose sweetener from starch in the 1600s. By 1782, people understood starches treated with acids could create a sweet substance. When sugar imports were blockaded during the Napoleonic Wars, several labs tried to develop alternative sweeteners. One success was dextrose, produced in 1801. Then in 1811, a Russian chemist accidentally overcooked potato starch and acid and wound up with glucose. He then developed a way to make a solid form of glucose. In 1878, another Russian chemist working in the United States made an accidental discovery. After a day of lab work, Constantin Fahlberg sat down to dinner, bit into a roll, and discovered it to be surprisingly sweet. Earlier, he had spilled an experimental compound over his hands. He rushed back to the lab, tasted everything, and discovered the source. An overboiled beaker had produced a chemical mixture that would become the artificial sweetener saccharin. After that, the development of sugar substitutes faded until the 1950s when HFCS was invented.

Some sugar substitutes are plant-based. Stevia (sold as Truvia, Pure Via, and Sun Crystals) is made from the stevia plant. Stevia is 300 times sweeter than sugar and does not contain calories.[9] Monk fruit, a melon from Central Asia, produces a sweetener sold as Nectresse. Its sweetness is 150 to 200 times greater than regular sugar.[10] Both monk fruit and stevia have received the GRAS approval from the FDA. However, they have not been studied in great detail.

SUGAR VERSUS SUGAR SUBSTITUTES

The first artificial sweetener was saccharin. Invented in 1878 and released a few years later, it quickly grew in popularity. It was not only used as a sweetener but was also prescribed for headaches and nausea. In 1906, Congress passed the Pure Food and Drug Act in an attempt to regulate the US food supply. The chemist in charge of enforcing the act recommended a ban on saccharin. However, President Theodore Roosevelt refused based on his personal experience. His physician had prescribed saccharin for weight loss, and Roosevelt had suffered no ill effects. Anecdotal evidence and public opinion often counted more than science when it came to regulating sweeteners. People concerned about their weight found the idea of eating sweets without calories appealing. They were willing to take some chances, if science could not prove with absolute certainty a substance was harmful. Government regulators and industry representatives continued to fight through the years. Saccharin was banned in processed foods, but it was still sold directly to consumers. Later saccharin was approved for use in processed foods as well.

In the early 1900s, saccharin entered use in many artificially sweetened food products.

In time, safety tests became more rigorous. Initially, a product was typically considered safe if it did not cause immediate, serious effects. By the 1950s, researchers were considering long-term effects and conducting studies on animals.

In the 1960s, many Americans concerned about their weight switched to drinking diet sodas. In five years, diet sodas went from 4 percent of the soft drink market to 15 percent.[11] Manufacturers benefited from the switch. Artificial sweeteners were cheaper than sugar, making diet drinks cheaper to produce.

Once again the sugar industry went to battle in the court of public opinion. It poured money into research studying any potential harmful effects of artificial sweeteners. Cyclamate sweeteners were banned after a study suggested they could cause bladder cancer in rats. Later evidence suggested that research was not relevant in humans. However, cyclamates are still banned from use in the United States.

In 1972, the FDA removed saccharin from the GRAS list in response to studies suggesting it might cause cancer in lab rats. The chemical companies manufacturing saccharin fought back, collecting evidence to support the safety of saccharin. They also waged a public opinion campaign, encouraging the public to protest government interference in their lives. Instead of a ban, the government declared saccharin products must carry a warning label. Sales of saccharin in the form of Sweet 'N Low rose greatly, perhaps in part because of all the publicity. The battle between sugar, HFCS, and sugar substitutes continues both in science and in public opinion. However, it will likely remain a large part of the US diet.

The name of one early diet soda, Slenderella, linked the drink with weight loss.

8 | A SWEET WORLD

Despite the challenges to sugar's supremacy as a sweetener, the sugar industry remains an important big business. Globally, more than 120 countries produce sugar.[1] Since 2010, annual production has varied between approximately 179 million short tons (162 million metric tons) and 196 million short tons (178 million metric tons).[2]

Sugar is a key crop in the United States and around the world. In the United States, more than 60,000 people are employed in the sugar industry.[3] Globally, millions of people depend on the sugar industry, including the growers, processors, and other industry workers, along with their dependents.

Worldwide, more than 50 million short tons (45 million metric tons) of sugar are imported and exported each year. Some countries cannot produce enough sugar to meet their own demand. For example, China's consumption of sugar for the 2016–2017 market season was predicted to be 17.8 million short tons (16.1 million metric tons). But the country produced only 8.2 million short tons (7.4 million metric tons), so the rest had to be supplied by imports.[4]

Sugar companies store and process huge quantities of sugar every day.

In other cases, a country may both import and export sugar. The European Union (EU) was expected to produce 16.1 million short tons (14.6 million metric tons) of sugar from sugar beets in the 2016–2017 market season.[5] Some of the sugar is used within the EU, and some is exported each year. The EU also imports raw cane sugar from other countries, primarily those that were once colonies of countries within the EU. If the EU did not export sugar, it would not need to import as much sugar to meet local demand. However, importing sugar acts as a form of foreign aid to the countries producing sugar. The United States also practices this form of aid, helping 40 countries through agreements to buy sugar in this way.[6]

In and Out

Brazil, India, and the EU have been the largest producers of sugar. China, which had been at number four, dropped into fifth place behind Thailand in 2015. The United States is the sixth-largest producer at approximately 8 million short tons (7.3 million metric tons), with imports of an additional 3 million short tons (2.7 million metric tons).[7] In terms of human consumption of sugar, India leads the world in total consumption. Although the amount consumed per person in India is low, the country has a large population and India exports sugar. The next areas of high total consumption are the EU, China, Brazil, and the United States.

PROVIDING SUPPORT

Many poorer, developing countries depend on exports of products such as sugar as a major part of their economies. This allows the countries that buy the product to influence the selling country in ways that go beyond simply paying money. For example, the EU developed a partnership agreement with developing countries. Known as the Cotonou Agreement, it went into effect in 2003 and expires in 2020. It applies to countries in Africa, the Caribbean, and the Pacific that are trading partners with the EU. The agreement addresses not only economic and trade cooperation, but also politics and local development. By the terms of the agreement, the EU helps its partners address security problems, avoid conflict, and build peace. It sets standards for addressing the problems of climate change, health concerns, and establishing a secure food supply. In this way the developing countries may receive political and social benefits along with a guaranteed price for their exports.

Agreements such as this can greatly benefit developing countrles. However, the process leaves them vulnerable to political upheaval. For example, sugar exports and tourism are the major industries in Fiji, a small country in the south Pacific Ocean. The EU is Fiji's most important economic partner. The EU promised to buy a certain amount of sugar at a fair price. In exchange Fiji committed to following certain rules regarding democratic principles and human rights. When a military coup took control of Fiji in December 2006, the new military government did not guarantee human rights or the rule of law. In return, the EU suspended support to Fiji, which led to falling sugar exports and rising unemployment. In circumstances such as these, the worldwide sugar industry can encourage developing countries to follow modern democratic principles. However, in the short term, citizens of those countries may suffer when support is withdrawn.

The example of Fiji also shows the risk facing any country that depends on a single crop for so much of its economy. When the demand for sugar is high, prices are high, and the country does well. However, if world sugar prices drop, that hurts the industry. If a country is dependent on the sugar industry, the whole country suffers. Guaranteed price supports from buyer countries can help even out the ups and downs of the sugar economy. Most trade agreements have limited

Mohammad Ahmad Khan is one of thousands of small sugarcane farmers in Fiji.

timeframes, however. The EU Common Agricultural Policy allowed certain developing countries to sell sugarcane to the EU with guaranteed high payments. This allowed the sugarcane to compete on price with local EU beet sugar. However, policy changes in 2017 meant the end of this special treatment. Without the guarantee of high prices, developing countries may not be able to sell their sugar at a profit in Europe.

PROTECTING US PRICES

Within each country, the government also plays a part in the sugar industry. Sugar grown in the United States typically costs more than sugar from other countries. The USDA has a complex loan program to guarantee sugar prices for US companies. Sugar processors use sugar as collateral when receiving loans from the USDA. In exchange, the processors must pay a certain minimum price to US sugar growers. When sugar prices are high, processors sell their product and repay the loan. If prices fall, the processing companies can forfeit the sugar to the government in exchange for forgiveness of the loan. In this way, the government guarantees prices for both sugar growers and sugar processors.

In addition, the government limits imports from certain other countries by restricting and taxing those imports. This results in higher prices for foreign sugar sold in the United States. Therefore, sugar from US growers can compete more easily

Trade Agreements

Global and regional trade agreements have many effects on the sugar industry. For example, the North American Free Trade Agreement (NAFTA) of 1994 allowed freer trade between the United States, Canada, and Mexico. The agreement does not directly allow for additional sugar imports from Canada. It does allow for easier importation of products containing sugar. Because sugar is cheaper in Canada, candy manufacturers can make their products more cheaply. This encouraged some companies to move their candy production from the United States to Canada.

US laws help keep
American farmers of sugar
beets and sugarcane
competitive with their
foreign counterparts.

on price. The US government even determines how much sugar should be produced in each state, and how much should come from sugar beets versus sugarcane.

While these policies benefit US sugar growers and processors, they harm others. When sugar prices are kept high, consumers pay more for sugar and for products containing sugar. Food manufacturers must pay higher prices for the sugar they use. Sugar industry jobs are protected, but jobs in food manufacturing may be lost. Some businesses have moved their factories abroad in order to have access to cheaper sugar. A report from the US Department of Commerce examined the effects of policies that keep US sugar prices high. The report found that for every job saved in sugar growing and harvesting, nearly three jobs were lost in US candy and sweets manufacturing.[8] Since the year 2000, several large companies have moved to Canada for access to cheaper sugar.

Some people and groups would like to see federal US sugar policy change. Opponents to current US sugar policy sometimes claim the government is unfairly choosing which companies win and which lose. They also complain about higher prices for businesses that use sugar and for consumers. Often these critics, such as the Sweetener Users Association, would benefit if sugar subsidies ended. A 2013 attempt to reduce sugar subsidies was voted down in the US Senate.

9 | HEALTHY LAND, HEALTHY PEOPLE

Politics and the sugar industry have an effect on nature as well. In the Florida Everglades, large areas have been converted to growing sugarcane. The cleared land has destroyed habitats for local animals. Many farmers use chemicals for fertilizers and pesticides, and these can also damage the environment. The Everglades are home to 77 endangered and threatened animals.[1] Many of these species are not found anywhere else in the United States.

The sugar industry is one of the biggest polluters in Florida, as well as one of the largest political donors. Sugar companies have donated millions of dollars to political candidates and parties. The Sugar Cane Growers Cooperative, US Sugar, and Florida Crystals are the major sugar industry players in Florida. After strong lobbying from the sugar industry, Florida lawmakers passed a bill to weaken pollution regulations.

Any industry has an effect on the environment. A product such as sugar affects the environment at several stages. Land may be cleared to plant sugarcane or sugar beets.

Pollution from sugar harvesting and processing has severely impacted the Everglades.

Smoke Complaints

In many places, including Hawaii and other US states, sugarcane is burned before harvesting. According to the sugar company HC&S, burning is necessary to remove the leafy part of the plant, so more sugar can be recovered from the stalk. The burning also destroys snakes and dangerous insects that could harm workers. However, if the burned material were left to rot, it could help enrich the soil. HC&S states it reduces its energy usage by not hauling and processing this material. Some plastic tubing is burned along with the cane, but the company says this is not harmful and it complies with all air quality regulations. However, any smoke can cause irritation in people who have respiratory problems. Some local people insisted they had health issues from cane burning. For financial reasons, HC&S shut down its sugarcane operations in 2016. It switched to a more diverse mix of food crops, energy crops, and cattle.

Clearing land can cause habitat destruction and deforestation. The water used on the crops may mean less water is available for other uses. Growers may use chemical fertilizers and pesticides on the crops, which can cause water pollution. Excessive use of chemicals can also pollute the soil and make it less fertile for future crops. Transporting and processing the sugarcane or beets into refined sugar uses energy and water.

Brazil's sugarcane industry has led to deforestation, but the nation is now taking steps to curb the damage.

Sugar has benefits over some other crops, and growers can follow guidelines and best practices to minimize pollution, conserve the environment, and even save money. Sugarcane can regrow for approximately six years, so the land does not need to be plowed every year. This reduces soil erosion and the need for fuel to run agricultural machinery. No-till farming techniques mean growers can avoid plowing even when fields need to be replanted. The use of bagasse for fuel means sugarcane

processing mills do not need to use fossil fuels. And using sugar for ethanol produces a fuel that is better for the environment than fossil fuels.

Climate Change

According to the Fairtrade Foundation, climate change is providing challenges to sugarcane farmers. Climate change increases extreme weather events, such as droughts, floods, and cyclones. These events can reduce the amount of sugarcane grown as well as interfere with storing, processing, and shipping the product. The World Bank, an international financial organization that provides loans to developing countries, conducted a four-year study of agricultural yields in India. The study concluded that sugarcane yields in one region could be reduced by up to 30 percent due to climate change.[2]

In Brazil, sugarcane farmers use few pesticides and almost no fungicides. They also breed the crop to withstand disease better. Environmentally friendly fertilizers replace most toxic industrial fertilizers. Diseases that threaten sugarcane are fought through biological control. Predator insects can consume prey insects that feed on plants. Parasites may also be used to kill insects. Disease-causing organisms such as bacteria and fungi destroy pest species too. All of these methods of pest control happen in nature. Farmers use biological control to increase the numbers and effectiveness of a pest's natural enemy.

To further protect the environment, the industry and government regulations can adopt environment-friendly policies. For example, the Brazilian government helps identify areas suitable for sugarcane. Government policies prohibit new sugarcane fields in sensitive ecosystems, such as the Amazon rain forest. Farmers are not allowed to destroy protected native plants to plant sugarcane fields. Sugarcane suppliers and processors have committed to protecting and recovering land alongside streams and riverbanks.

SMALL FARM CHALLENGES

Human health, safety, and quality of life are also affected by industry and political policies. Although large businesses control most of the sugar sales, many growers on small farms produce sugar. The small-scale farmers may own their own land, or the local sugar processing mill may own the land they farm. The farmers grow the sugarcane, harvest it, and deliver it to a local mill.

Harvesting and processing sugar can be strenuous, dangerous work. Sugarcane cutters often use machetes, which can result in cuts, repetitive use injuries, and even severed limbs. The tough cane stalks can also cause cuts and eye injuries. Exposure to heat and sun can cause skin cancer and heat exhaustion. Using pesticides and inhaling smoke from cane burning can damage skin, eyes, and the respiratory system. Some sugarcane workers are seasonal migrants who may have to live in crowded, unsanitary company housing. In a number of countries, child labor is used in the sugarcane fields.

In the United States, the sugar industry is made up largely of farmer-owned cooperatives. These organizations collectively own multiple farms and processing facilities. They work with refineries and other companies to ship the sugar from the farms to store shelves.

Fair Trade Labeling

Several organizations set standards for fair trade labeling in different countries. Fairtrade International coordinates the labeling system at the international level. Fair trade groups set and review standards to determine the best fair trade practices for each industry. Sugarcane producers can band together in producer organizations. They must act on democratic principles, with each member having an equal vote. Child labor and forced labor are prohibited. Environmental standards consider the best practices to protect the fields and the surrounding environment. In exchange, the fair trade organizations offer loans and advice. Some growers are using the financial support and cooperation of the fair trade movement to expand their businesses. In Paraguay, one cooperative built its own sugar processing mill. This keeps more of the sugar industry money in the hands of the growers.

Globally, sugar farmers often live in poverty. Processing and marketing are done by large corporations who also receive most of the profit. A mere six companies account for approximately two-thirds of the world trade in sugar.[3] The international trade laws that affect sugar can make it difficult for small farmers to sell their sugar for a good price.

A policy called fair trade can help. This international movement aims to reduce poverty by helping farmers. Fair trade standards address prices, worker pay, health and safety, and living conditions for workers. Fair trade sugar aims to improve the position of small-scale sugarcane growers. It develops partnerships among farmers and cane processors, hoping to provide access to international markets.

Consumers who buy sugar or sugar products that are certified fair-trade pay a premium to support ethical standards. For sugar, 99 farmers' organizations represent more than 62,000 small sugarcane farmers internationally.[4] In the United States, several companies provide fair trade–certified organic sugar. Additional products, such as chocolates, may also be made with fair trade sugar.

The price of fair trade sugar is negotiated between producers and traders. Traders pay an additional premium to get certified fair trade sugar. Some of this extra income goes directly to the farmers. The rest is used to improve facilities or provide tools and training. In some countries, the plan has helped build schools or provide electricity or water to communities. According to the Fairtrade Foundation, many companies are making the commitment to use sugar produced by these standards.

Alfredo Ortega, part of the Belize Sugar Cane Farmers Association, commented on the changes these standards brought: "Fairtrade is like a door to a great opportunity within our community. . . . Through the social programme, Fairtrade can help us promote education and build schools, health centres, clinics and much more. For us, Fairtrade has been a new beginning and also encourages a strong future in the sugar industry."[5]

THE FUTURE OF SUGAR

Able to not only sweeten snacks and drinks, but also fuel cars and bring countries energy independence, sugar is one of today's most versatile and important commodities. The health consequences of sugar overconsumption have become well known, but the sweet substance

continues to be championed by trade groups and food corporations, and consumers continue to buy it in mass quantities.

Sugar has a major impact on the world economy. It drives billions of dollars in sales of snacks and beverages, and nations around the world produce, process, and transport millions of tons of it each year. Sugar, once called "white gold" by North American plantation owners, remains a critical crop in today's world.

SUGARCANE PRODUCTION 2014[6]

MEXICO
62,471,100 short tons
(56,672,829 metric tons)

COLOMBIA
42,061,037 short tons
(38,157,131 metric tons)

BRAZIL
812,575,092 short tons
(737,155,724 metric tons)

N
W ✦ E
S

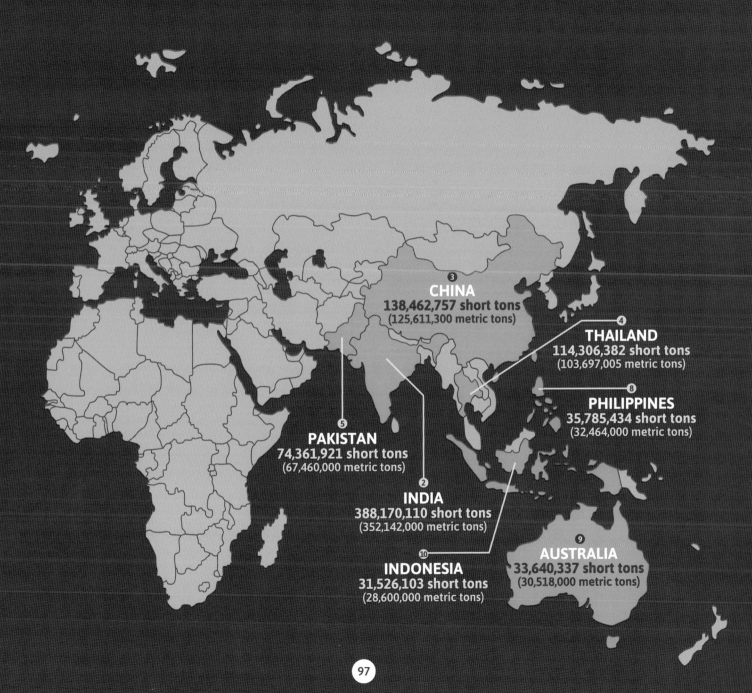

CHINA
138,462,757 short tons
(125,611,300 metric tons)

THAILAND
114,306,382 short tons
(103,697,005 metric tons)

PHILIPPINES
35,785,434 short tons
(32,464,000 metric tons)

PAKISTAN
74,361,921 short tons
(67,460,000 metric tons)

INDIA
388,170,110 short tons
(352,142,000 metric tons)

AUSTRALIA
33,640,337 short tons
(30,518,000 metric tons)

INDONESIA
31,526,103 short tons
(28,600,000 metric tons)

Timeline

500 BCE
People in India learn how to refine sugar from sugarcane stalks.

642 CE
The Arabs invade Persia, uncover the technique of refining sugar, and spread it throughout their empire.

1199
Sugar is first mentioned in England.

1493
Christopher Columbus brings sugarcane to the West Indies.

1747
A method of extracting sugar from beets is discovered in Berlin.

1793–1815
The British Navy blockades French ports during the Napoleonic Wars, stopping the import of sugar and other goods.

1874
The English sugar tax is removed, lowering prices and leading to more widespread sugar consumption.

1880
Beets become the primary source of sugar in Europe.

1934
The Jones-Costigan Sugar Act establishes US sugar policy.

1943
Companies in the US sugar industry found the Sugar Research Foundation.

1947

The Sugar Research Foundation is renamed the Sugar Association.

1976

The US Food and Drug Administration declares sugar generally recognized as safe and not a hazard to the public.

1977

A government Select Committee on Nutrition and Human Needs recommends that Americans lower their sugar intake by 40 percent.

1994

The North American Free Trade Agreement allows freer trade between the United States, Canada, and Mexico, including easier importation of products containing sugar.

2003

The World Health Organization (WHO) recommends that people should get no more than 10 percent of their calories from added sugars, but it drops the recommendation from the official report after threats to cut off funding to WHO.

2012

Scientists from the University of California, San Francisco release an article suggesting that sugar is addictive and should be regulated in the way alcohol and tobacco are.

2013

An attempt to reduce US sugar policy is voted down in the US Senate.

2015

A scientific advisory committee recommends that the 2015–2020 Dietary Guidelines for Americans suggest people keep added sugars to no more than 10 percent of their diets.

Essential Facts

IMPACT ON HISTORY

The demand for sugar was a major cause of the transatlantic slave trade. More than 12.5 million enslaved people were shipped from Africa to the Americas between 1501 and 1867. Half of them worked on sugarcane plantations. Sugar consumption has grown dramatically in the last two centuries. Some experts believe that this may be the cause of rising rates of obesity, type 2 diabetes, heart disease, and other health problems. As of 2014, sugarcane is the third most valuable crop in the world, after cereal grains and rice.

KEY FIGURES

▶ The Persian Emperor Darius invaded India in 510 BCE and learned about sugarcane. The Persians used sugar but kept the method of producing sugar from sugarcane a secret.

▶ The Sugar Association, a sugar industry group, promotes sugar to the public in the United States. The World Sugar Research Organisation does the same worldwide.

▶ The European Union has a role in the worldwide sugar industry through the Cotonou Agreement. In effect from 2003 to 2020, the agreement addresses economic and trade cooperation, politics, and local development for many EU trading partners.

▶ The US government supports US sugar growers and sugar processers by guaranteeing sugar prices for US companies.

KEY STATISTICS

▶ Sugarcane takes between six and 24 months to reach maturity, with an average time of 12 months.

▶ Globally, more than 120 countries produce sugar.

▶ Approximately 80 percent of global sugar comes from sugarcane, with the rest from sugar beets.

▶ In the United States, more than 60,000 people are employed in the sugar industry.

QUOTE

"We see ethanol as the fuel of the future, whether it's in Brazil or in the world beyond."

—Abel Uchoa, manager at a Brazil sugarcane company

Glossary

antioxidant

A substance in food that prevents harmful chemical reactions involving oxygen.

bagasse

The waste product left over from sugarcane processing, which can be burned as fuel.

biological control

The reduction of harmful pest populations by introducing natural enemies of those pests into the environment.

blood sugar

The concentration of glucose in the blood, produced by the body from food.

commodity

Something that has value and is bought and sold.

ferment

A chemical change, often involving yeast or microorganisms, that results in the production of alcohol.

fossil fuel

A natural fuel, such as coal or gas, which contributes to global climate change.

fungicide

A chemical that destroys fungus and is used to protect plants.

greenhouse gas

A gas that absorbs infrared radiation and traps heat in the atmosphere.

HDL cholesterol

High-density lipoprotein cholesterol, a beneficial substance that helps remove harmful low-density lipoprotein cholesterol from the body.

lobbying

Trying to convince government officials to vote in a certain way.

machete

A broad, heavy knife that may be used as a weapon or to clear brush or sugarcane.

metabolize

To change by metabolism, the physical and chemical means by which an organism processes energy.

pesticide

A substance or chemical used to destroy insects or other organisms that are harmful to cultivated plants.

rationing

Setting limits on the amount of certain foods or materials a population can purchase during war or other conflicts.

subsidy

Money paid, usually by a government, to keep the price of a product or service low.

Additional Resources

SELECTED BIBLIOGRAPHY

Cohen, Rich. "Sugar Love." *National Geographic*. National Geographic, Aug. 2013. Web. 23 Aug. 2016.

Engber, Daniel. "Dark Sugar." *Slate*. Slate, 28 Apr. 2009. Web. 23 Aug. 2016.

FURTHER READINGS

Aronson, Marc, and Marina Budhos. *Sugar Changed the World: A Story of Magic, Spice, Slavery, Freedom, and Science*. Boston, MA: Clarion, 2010. Print.

FOR MORE INFORMATION

For more information on this subject, contact or visit the following organizations:

Southdown Plantation House and The Terrebonne Museum

1208 Museum Drive
Houma, LA 70360
985-851-0154
http://www.southdownmuseum.org/

This sugar manor house dating to the 1800s houses a museum of history and culture.

Sugarland Tours

109 Central Avenue
Clewiston, FL 33440
863-983-7979
http://www.clewiston.org/

Heritage and agricultural tours provide a look at a sugarcane farm and sugar mill.

Source Notes

CHAPTER 1. FUELED BY SUGAR

1. Aurelie Mejean and Chris Hope. "Modeling the Costs of Energy Crops: A Case Study of US Corn and Brazilian Sugarcane." *Energy Policy* 38 (2010): 547-561. Web. 11 May 2016.

2. "Ethanol." *SugarCane.org*. SugarCane.org, 2016. Web. 24 Aug. 2016.

3. José Goldemberg and Luiz A. Horta Nogueira. "Sweetening the Biofuel Sector: The History of Sugarcane Ethanol in Brazil." *Bioenergy Connection*. Bioenergy Connection, Fall 2014. Web. 9 May 2016.

4. Juan Forero. "Brazil's Ethanol Sector, Once Thriving, Is Being Buffeted by Forces Both Man-Made, Natural." *Washington Post*. Washington Post, 1 Jan. 2014.

5. José Goldemberg and Luiz A. Horta Nogueira. "Sweetening the Biofuel Sector: The History of Sugarcane Ethanol in Brazil." *Bioenergy Connection*. Bioenergy Connection, Fall 2014. Web. 9 May 2016.

6. "What Is Bagasse?" *Eco Kloud*. Eco Kloud, n.d. Web. 9 May 2016.

7. "Bioplastics." *SugarCane.org*. SugarCane.org, 2016. Web. 24 Aug. 2016.

8. José Goldemberg and Luiz A. Horta Nogueira. "Sweetening the Biofuel Sector: The History of Sugarcane Ethanol in Brazil." *Bioenergy Connection*. Bioenergy Connection, Fall 2014. Web. 9 May 2016.

9. "World Sugar Production." *Sucden*. Sucden, n.d. Web. 24 Aug. 2016.

CHAPTER 2. THE RISE OF SUGARCANE

1. Howard Belton. *A History of the World in Five Menus*. Bloomington, IN: Author House, 2015. Google Books. 16 May 2016.

2. "How Sugar Is Made—The History." *Sucrose.org*. Sucrose.org, n.d. Web. 24 Aug. 2016.

3. "Abolition of Slavery in the Americas." *International Slavery Museum*. International Slavery Museum, 2016. Web. 24 Aug. 2016.

4. "History of Sugar." *Sugar Nutrition UK*. Sugar Nutrition UK, n.d. Web. 16 May 2016.

5. Rich Cohen. "Sugar Love." *National Geographic*. National Geographic, Aug. 2013. Web. 24 Aug. 2016.

6. Ibid.

7. Mark Horton, Alexander Bentley, and Philip Langton. "A History of Sugar—The Food Nobody Needs, but Everyone Craves." *IFL Science*. IFL Science, 1 Nov. 2015. Web. 24 Aug. 2016.

8. Joseph Nordqvist. "How Much Sugar Is in Your Food and Drink?" *Medical News Today*. MNT, 19 Nov. 2015. Web. 24 Aug. 2016.

9. "Sugar: World Markets and Trade." *USDA*. USDA, Nov. 2015. Web. 24 Aug. 2016.

10. Ibid.

11. "About Sugar." *Fair Trade Foundation*. Fair Trade Foundation, n.d. Web. 24 Aug. 2016.

12. Ibid.

13. Roberto A. Ferdman. "Where People around the World Eat the Most Sugar and Fat." *Washington Post*. Washington Post, 5 Feb. 2015. Web. 24 Aug. 2016.

CHAPTER 3. A NEW SOURCE OF SWEETNESS

1. Tori Avey. "Discover the History of Beets." *PBS Food*. PBS, 8 Oct. 2014. Web. 24 Aug. 2016.

2. "Slavery Today." *Free the Slaves*. Free the Slaves, 2016. Web. 24 Aug. 2016.

3. Tori Avey. "Discover the History of Beets." *PBS Food*. PBS, 8 Oct. 2014. Web. 24 Aug. 2016.

4. "Molasses." *How Products Are Made*. How Products Are Made, n.d. Web. 17 May 2016.

5. "A Sticky Tragedy: The Boston Molasses Disaster." *History Today*. History Today, 1 Jan. 2009. Web. 24 Aug. 2016.

6. Ibid.

CHAPTER 4. THE SCIENCE OF SWEET

1. "The Other 26 Sweeteners." *Sugar Association*. Sugar Association, n.d. Web. 17 May 2016.

2. "Added Sugars: Don't Get Sabotaged by Sweeteners." *Mayo Clinic*. Mayo Clinic, n.d. Web. 24 Aug. 2016.

3. Laura Moss. "Do Foods Taste the Same to Animals as They Do to Us?" *Mother Nature Network*. Mother Nature Network, 29 Sept. 2014. Web. 18 May 2016.

4. "Added Sugars: Don't Get Sabotaged by Sweeteners." *Mayo Clinic*. Mayo Clinic, n.d. Web. 24 Aug. 2016.

CHAPTER 5. SELLING SUGAR

1. "About Us." *Sugar Association*. Sugar Association, n.d. Web. 19 May 2016.

2. Maddie Oatman. "A Timeline of Sugar Spin." *Mother Jones*. Mother Jones, 31 Oct. 2012. Web. 24 Aug. 2016.

3. Ibid.

4. "Careers." *US Sugar*. US Sugar, n.d. Web. 24 Aug. 2016.

5. "Reversing the Epidemic." *New York City Obesity Task Force*. New York City Obesity Task Force, 31 May 2012. Web. 19 May 2016.

6. Brooke Metz. "Less Is More: For Coca-Cola, Small Packs Mean Big Business." 22 July 2015. Web. 24 Aug. 2016.

7. Ted Ryan. "11 Facts About the Coca-Cola Bottle." *Coca-Cola Company*. Coca-Cola Company, 26 Feb. 2015. Web. 24 Aug. 2016.

8. Brooke Metz. "Less Is More: For Coca-Cola, Small Packs Mean Big Business." 22 July 2015. Web. 24 Aug. 2016.

9. "Reversing the Epidemic." *New York City Obesity Task Force*. New York City Obesity Task Force, 31 May 2012. Web. 19 May 2016.

10. Tom Webb. "King-Sized Snickers, Other Candy Bars Slimming Down." *Pioneer Press*. Pioneer Press, 15 Feb. 2012. Web. 24 Aug. 2016.

11. Maddie Oatman. "A Timeline of Sugar Spin." *Mother Jones*. Mother Jones, 31 Oct. 2012. Web. 24 Aug. 2016.

12. "Our World." *ASR Group*. ASR Group, n.d. Web. 24 Aug. 2016.

Source Notes Continued

13. "Our Owners." *ASR Group*. ASR Group, n.d. Web. 24 Aug. 2016.

14. Gary Taubes and Cristin Kearns Couzens. "Big Sugar's Sweet Little Lies." *Mother Jones*. Mother Jones, Nov./Dec. 2012. Web. 24 Aug. 2016.

15. Ibid.

16. Ibid.

17. Ibid.

18. "Dietary Guidelines for Americans 2015–2020." *Health.gov*. Health.gov, 2015. Web. 24 Aug. 2016.

19. Gary Taubes and Cristin Kearns Couzens. "Big Sugar's Sweet Little Lies." *Mother Jones*. Mother Jones, Nov./Dec. 2012. Web. 24 Aug. 2016.

CHAPTER 6. SUGAR AND HEALTH

1. Christian Nordqvist. "What Is Sugar? How Much Added Sugar Should I Have?" *Medical News Today*. Medical News Today, 17 Sept. 2014. Web. 24 Aug. 2016.

2. "Reversing the Epidemic." *New York City Obesity Task Force*. New York City Obesity Task Force, 31 May 2012. Web. 19 May 2016.

3. "Obesity Facts." *CDC*. CDC, n.d. Web. 24 Aug. 2016.

4. "Reversing the Epidemic." *New York City Obesity Task Force*. New York City Obesity Task Force, 31 May 2012. Web. 19 May 2016.

5. Maddie Oatman. "The Health Effects of Sugar. Is Sugar as Addictive as Alcohol?" *Mother Jones*. Mother Jones. 2 Feb. 2012. Web. 24 Aug. 2016.

CHAPTER 7. FACING OFF AGAINST OTHER SWEETENERS

1. Ali Morse and Dr. LeFebure. "History of High-Fructose Corn Syrup." *Cluster Seven-Biomedical Sciences*. UC Davis, 30 July 2012. Web. 24 Aug. 2016.

2. Daniel Engber. "Dark Sugar." *Slate*. Slate, 28 Apr. 2009. Web. 24 Aug. 2016.

3. Gary Taubes. "Is Sugar Toxic?" *New York Times Magazine*. New York Times Magazine, 13 Apr. 2011. Web. 24 Aug. 2016.

4. Michael M. Landa. "Response to Petition from Corn Refiners Association to Authorize 'Corn Sugar' as an Alternate Common or Usual Name for High Fructose Corn Syrup (HFCS)." *FDA*. FDA, 30 May 2012. Web. 24 Aug. 2016. FDA. Web. May 25, 2016.

5. Dana Milbank. "The Sugar Lobby's Sour Tactics." *Washington Post*. Washington Post, 10 Apr. 2015. Web. 24 Aug. 2016.

6. "Dietary Guidelines for Americans 2015–2020." *Health.gov*. Health.gov, 2015. Web. 24 Aug. 2016.

7. Kiera Butler. "Is Sugar Really Healthier Than Corn Syrup?" *Mother Jones*. Mother Jones, 14 Mar. 2011. Web. 24 Aug. 2016.

8. "Sweeteners—Sugar Substitutes." *MEDLINEplus*. NIH, n.d. Web. 24 Aug. 2016.

9. Bridget Murray Law. "New Sweetener Not So Sweet for Your Diet." *NBC News*. NBC, 17 Apr. 2009. Web. 26 May 2016.

10. "Sweeteners—Sugar Substitutes." *MEDLINEplus*. NIH, n.d. Web. 24 Aug. 2016.

11. Gary Taubes and Cristin Kearns Couzens. "Big Sugar's Sweet Little Lies." *Mother Jones*. Mother Jones, Nov./Dec. 2012. Web. 24 Aug. 2016.

CHAPTER 8. A SWEET WORLD

1. "Fair Trade and Sugar." *Fairtrade International.* Fairtrade International, n.d. Web. 27 May 2016.

2. "Sugar: World Markets and Trade." *USDA.* USDA, n.d. Web. 27 May 2016.

3. Chris Edwards. "The Sugar Racket." *Cato Institute.* Cato Institute, June 2007. Web. 26 May 2016.

4. "Sugar: World Markets and Trade." *USDA.* USDA, n.d. Web. 27 May 2016.

5. Shelley Goldberg. "The Commodities Market Has a Sweet Tooth." *Wall Street Daily.* Wall Street Daily, 26 May 2016. Web. 24 Aug. 2016.

6. "Sugar Industry." *International Encyclopedia of the Social Sciences.* Encyclopedia.com, 2008. Web. 24 Aug. 2016.

7. "Sugar: World Markets and Trade." *USDA.* USDA, n.d. Web. 27 May 2016.

8. "Employment Changes in US Food Manufacturing: The Impact of Sugar Prices." *International Trade Administration.* International Trade Administration, n.d. Web. 24 Aug. 2016.

CHAPTER 9. HEALTHY LAND, HEALTHY PEOPLE

1. Dexter Filkins. "Swamped." *New Yorker.* New Yorker, 4 Jan. 2016. Web. 24 Aug. 2016.

2. "Fair Trade and Sugar." *Fairtrade International.* Fairtrade International, n.d. Web. 24 Aug. 2016.

3. Ibid.

4. "About Sugar." *Fairtrade Foundation.* Fairtrade Foundation, n.d. Web. 24 Aug. 2016.

5. "Fair Trade and Sugar." *Fairtrade International.* Fairtrade International, n.d. Web. 24 Aug. 2016.

6. "Production Quantities by Country, 2014—Sugar Cane." *Food and Agriculture Organization of the United Nations, Statistics Division.* United Nations, 2015. Web. 26 Aug. 2016.

Index

Achard, Franz, 28

American Heart Association, 40

artificial sweeteners, 34, 72–76

ASR Group, 48

dextrose, 33–34, 70, 72, 73

diabetes, 47, 49, 51, 55, 59, 60, 72

dietary guidelines, 40, 51, 71

ethanol, 7–9, 13, 90

Hawaii, 44, 88

heart disease, 47, 51, 55, 57–60

high-fructose corn syrup, 33, 36, 57, 60, 67–71, 72, 73, 76

obesity, 44, 55–57, 60, 69
Ortega, Alfredo, 93

Papua New Guinea, 15
Persia, 16
pesticides, 70, 87–91
Pure Food and Drug Act, 74

Roosevelt, Theodore, 74

saccharine, 72, 73, 74, 76
slavery, 17–19, 28
soda, 5, 16, 20, 40–41, 47, 60, 70, 75
sucrose, 23, 33, 72
sugar
    addiction, 63
    consumption levels, 19–20, 40–41,
        51, 69
    in foods, 5, 13, 20, 33, 40–41, 46
    health effects, 47, 49, 51–53, 55–65
    history, 15–19, 43–53
    medical use, 17, 34
    taste, 38, 40, 62
    types, 23

sugar alcohols, 34, 73
Sugar Association, 44, 46, 47, 49,
    50–51, 69, 71
sugar beets
    growing, 27–29, 31
    harvesting, 28
    processing, 27–29, 31
sugarcane
    environmental impact, 87–91
    growing, 20–23, 24
    harvesting, 24
    processing, 24–25

triangle trade, 19

United Kingdom, 19
United States, 7, 8, 9, 12, 23, 27, 28, 55,
    59, 76, 80, 93
    sugar jobs, 79, 85
    sugar policies, 17, 43, 44, 83, 85
US Sugar Corporation, 45

volatile compounds, 38

West Indies, 17, 28
World Health Organization, 53
World Sugar Research
    Organisation, 44
World War I, 43
World War II, 43, 44

ABOUT THE AUTHOR

M. M. Eboch writes about science, history, and culture for all ages. Her recent nonfiction titles include *Chaco Canyon*, *Living with Dyslexia*, and *The Green Movement*. She writes fiction as Chris Eboch. Her novels for young people include *The Genie's Gift*, a Middle Eastern fantasy; *The Eyes of Pharaoh*, a mystery in ancient Egypt; *The Well of Sacrifice*, a Mayan adventure; and the Haunted series, which starts with *The Ghost on the Stairs*.

DATE DUE